Liberation

Contributors and Supporting Organisation:

The Leukaemia Foundation of Australia.
230 Lutwyche Road, Windsor QLD 4030

> '*A story of a beautiful woman full of life, and her fight against a deady disease, with the power she gained to overcome it.*'
>
> —Dr Rajesperasingam

> '*I couldn't put it down! This will help many people and open the eyes of others as well.*'
>
> —Sarah O'Brien

Liberation

BREAKING THE CHAINS TO SURVIVAL AND
FREEDOM – A TRUE STORY

KARINA CARREL

BALBOA.
PRESS

A DIVISION OF HAY HOUSE

Edited by:
Christine Nagel Literary Services
christine.nagel@bigpond.com
0417 092 332

Balboa Press books may be ordered through booksellers or by contacting:

Balboa Press
A Division of Hay House
1663 Liberty Drive
Bloomington, IN 47403
www.balboapress.com.au
1-(877) 407-4847

ISBN: 978-1-4525-0958-7 (sc)
ISBN: 978-1-4525-0964-8 (e)

Front cover design: Karina Carrel and Paul Carrel
Ribbon design: Karina Carrel and Paul Carrel
Graphics: Rimma Campos
Author photograph by: Aaliyah Carrel

Printed in the United States of America

Balboa Press rev. date: 05/02/2013

For my Children

In the time I was down and reaching my end
Drowning deep into a despair that would send
All of us spiralling into a place
Of pain staring cancer in the face

You saw through the hurt of my tortured soul
Filled with the pain, you tore down that wall
With an unconditional love to heal
You brought me back to life, to feel

To my three angels, you saved me
From fading and giving in to the sea
Of darkness that battered and bruised my being
You pulled me through to the light, seeing

I'm alive and breathing because of you
I survived its wrath because of you
I am stronger now because of you
The pieces are back together, because of you.

INTRODUCTION

This is not just a story—this is my personal cancer journey. My name is Karina and I'm a proud Hodgkin's Lymphoma survivor. Thousands of people around the world are fighting or have survived both Hodgkin's or non-Hodgkin's lymphoma. Thousands have also lost their lives to this type of blood cancer that you never really hear of. Lymphoma is the sixth most common cancer in Australia, but it is overlooked on a global scale.

Sadly, in some cases, it can take a lymphoma patient anywhere from six months to a year, or sometimes even longer, to discover their tumours. The symptoms it carries are often ignored, simply because there is not enough awareness of it.

In Australia, an estimated thirty-one people each day are diagnosed with blood cancers, which claim more lives each year than the better-known cancers. As blood cancers are the second biggest cause of cancer in our country, more awareness is imperative.

Before and during my experience I researched the internet but I could only ever find medical information filled with complicated terminology. It would only confuse me more than I already was and scare me beyond mere fear. I'd get impatient reading things written in point form or essay length reports in what seemed like another language.

I craved personal details. I wanted to read the experiences from a cancer fighter's point of view: real human beings expressing real human emotions, not text book descriptions.

My mission is to shine a light on lymphoma—to bring about the recognition and understanding that is needed: that this disease is just as serious as other cancers—to give all of who have fallen to it a voice.

I have written about my journey with honesty and in detail. My hope is to help cancer patients who are going through, or about to embark on, their own cancer journey—that they may find some ease, hope and strength through my words. Although every cancer journey is different and unique, the emotions and physical changes are similar, no matter what type of cancer we battle. Somehow we are all connected through the same fight: our fight for life.

I also hope to provide some knowledge for each person involved—supporters and loved ones—to gain a better understanding of what many of us may go through in our silent times. Because sometimes with knowledge comes comfort.

Going through a journey with cancer can be hard. Harder than people could ever imagine. The word 'cancer' alone used to send gut wrenching shivers down my spine. Now it's become a part of my reality. To go through the illness and months of not knowing what to expect at the end of it all, can be mentally and physically exhausting, creating emotional distress for not only the patient, but everyone else involved.

Being a mother and having a family put extra pressure on me to try to lead a normal life. On the days that I was feeling like a train wreck, like I'd been run over by a semi-trailer, I wouldn't tell anyone and pretend I was fine. I was perpetually worried about my children and my family.

My three children are the absolute world to me. If anything were to happen to any of us, it would be my worst nightmare. Yes, they can drive us crazy and our house can often be mistaken for a circus, but I love my family.

It was hard enough for them to watch me go through so many physical changes, so I'd hide my raw emotions and deal with them in my own time and anywhere I could—in the shower, on the toilet, even while driving, wherever I found the time to be alone. Not wanting to burden my family with my problems, I doubted my own self worth, absurdly consumed with guilt for putting my family through the trials of having cancer.

In hindsight, I think pretending to be fine was what 'saved' me, so to speak, because pretending would eventually turn into optimism and strength, by making a promise to myself to do anything and conquer anything. Eventually, I would become my own unstoppable super hero, developing tunnel vision, entirely focused on the end result. Giving in to cancer and everything that comes with it wasn't an option. Liberation was my quest.

My husband Paul and I always knew we were destined to be together. We had our children early and didn't feel the need to rush into marriage. We went against everything traditional and did it all backwards. It took us eight years to make 'us' official and get married.

It seemed our lives were on the right track. We felt blessed. There were no problems or dramas in our lives, and even though Paul and I were in love, we became a bit, well, monotonous. After being together for ten years I thought that was normal.

In the months to follow, I would only dream about having that monotony back.

Before my illness, we lived with my parents. My father had been going through some serious health problems and needed my care. Little did we know at the time that I would be the one needing the help.

Around that time I saw documentaries about mothers going through chemotherapy and looking after their children during their 'dark' days. They'd describe those days as hell on earth, when the chemotherapy took its toll on the body and when the fatigue of treatment along with a roller coaster of emotions took over.

Those women and their stories would affect me for days. Even through their sadness, they were so inspiring to me. Instead of letting the sadness take over, they would simply push themselves to change their mind-set and enjoy the smallest of moments with their kids. As difficult as it looked to be in that situation, they always managed a smile.

I remember thinking, 'I hope that never happens to me. I hope I never get cancer.' I didn't know what was more terrifying, cancer or chemo. I was simply an outsider, someone that didn't understand anything about cancer and who took life for granted. Without knowing it at the time, those documentaries opened my eyes for what lay ahead of me.

Without a doubt, chemotherapy was a time of crisis for my family and me. However, we all took it as it came, adapting ourselves around a new life with cancer. Then we readjusted to life after cancer when the treatment was over with the understanding that everything could change in a blink of an eye.

I have my battle scars and chemo stripes, and I wear them with pride, embracing survivorship and the gift of life. Taking each day as it comes, I now have a different perspective: what it means to be alive and live in the moment. Cancer changed me emotionally, mentally, physically and spiritually. I know my truth. I know my pain. I know the extent of my strength.

Renouncing my spirit at the beginning of my journey would have created a different outcome, but I'm a cancer survivor, and I'm proud of what I went through. This is my new normal, and that is all that matters.

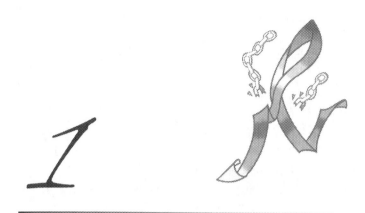

FINDING THE EXTENT OF YOUR STRENGTH

March 2009

Soon after giving birth to my third child, my beautiful son, in February 2009, very small symptoms started to appear.

I knew something was wrong, but at the same time I didn't understand what was happening to me.

I cherished being a stay at home mum. Looking after my newborn baby boy while my daughters were in school was the highlight of my day. Having the two older girls, (Aaliyah. aged seven and Monique. aged six), and watching them grow so fast, I knew that every minute at home with him was precious. This time around, I was determined to appreciate all the special moments of being a mother with my baby—the good times along with the tough times.

Wanting to give him the best of everything from the day he was born, I decided to express milk for him, as breast-feeding was never easy for me.

I had developed mastitis twice by the time he was four weeks old. Even though I'd had it before, there was something different about the infection this time. I felt a 'pulling' sensation in my chest and it didn't seem right to me. It was a tightness starting from my jawline, running down the side of my neck to the left side of my chest. I'd feel it when I lifted my chin up towards the ceiling. This was something I'd never felt before? Or was it?

I kept looking up to the ceiling and prodding that part of my neck, but I couldn't feel anything with my fingers. Was that feeling supposed to be there? I convinced myself it was part of the infection. I took antibiotics and trusted my body to get back to normal quickly. It always did.

This time would be different.

April 2009

I started feeling the 'pull' more often, sometimes daily, especially while taking a shower and washing my neck. The infection was gone, but this pulling sensation was still inside my chest. It was then that I began to worry, and for a split second I wondered if it could be breast cancer.

I laughed at myself. Although the pull was slightly near my breast, the sensation was strongest down my neck so it couldn't be breast cancer. Feeling like an idiot, I mentally slapped myself upside the head and told myself to stop being a drama queen.

I researched some websites about mastitis to find out what could be creating this sensation. The information gave the impression that tightness and pressure in the chest and neck areas were typical symptoms and after effects that could sometimes last for weeks after the infection had been cured. I relaxed.

After a few days, the fact that the pulling was still there bothered me, and alarm bells began ringing. Something just didn't feel right. I went to my GP to ask his advice, also asking for an X-ray for my own peace of mind. Unfortunately, I couldn't have an X-ray as I was still expressing. However, the doctor reassured me that the tightness would eventually stop on its own within a week or two.

Two weeks later I stopped expressing milk as the pull was becoming uncomfortable. Even so, I ignored it.

July 2009

After my son had turned five months old, I began feeling the sensation a lot more, along with a firm pushing sensation against my throat on the same left side, especially when stretching my arms above my head. The weird part was that I hadn't expressed milk for over two months. Surely it couldn't be the after effects of the mastitis.

When I went back to the doctor, he examined me and told me everything seemed fine and not to worry. He felt my neck and the whole area around my left shoulder and chest and gave me the all-clear. There was nothing out of the ordinary. The verdict was that my breast tissue was still recovering from the mastitis.

Life continued, with the dreaded morning routine of getting the kids ready for school, repeating myself 50 million times before 9 am: 'Eat your breakfast, swallow your food, get dressed, brush your teeth, stop fighting.' Oh, the headache. Then drive to school like a maniac because we were always running late. I'd spend the rest of the day looking after my son, living an uneventful life.

Craving a break from monotony, I joined an aerobics class, desperate to lose the massive 37 kg I'd gained during my last pregnancy. It felt good to have time to myself, even if only for an hour. Strange things started happening soon after the warm up. Not only did I feel the tightness and the 'pull' a lot stronger than usual, but I couldn't breathe! Something was constricting my natural ability to take in a deep breath!

The room started spinning, as I couldn't get any air! I was suffocating, but from what? Feeling like my food was about to be sprayed all over the floor, I grabbed my bag and ran out of the room. As I tried to get some oxygen in and open my lungs, I started panicking. All of a sudden, I had a sharp stabbing pain through the left side of my upper body, to the middle of my back. I wrenched the neck of my shirt, desperate for air. Had I pulled a muscle or was I having a heart attack?

I grabbed my Ventolin and tried to calm myself down, because panicking wasn't helping. Slowly, through the rasping in my throat, my breath came back. I told myself that I couldn't breathe because I was overweight. That was it. Completely embarrassed, I went home.

But something was definitely wrong: in the shower I checked for the tightness again. Yes, it was still there, but it was now joined by a sharp pain in the left side of my chest. Just to test myself, I tried to take a deep breath in, but found that the breath became obstructed halfway. With it, pain stabbed through my spine. I had a sinking feeling in the pit of my stomach.

During all this time, there had been a constant fist of pressure against my neck, but only then did I realise it. Still, in the throes of denial, I told myself once again that I was being stupid.

August 2009

About a week later I developed a cold and an irritating dry cough I couldn't seem shake. The cough prevented me from speaking normally, ending all of my sentences, and the syrups didn't do a thing.

That weekend I went to see Pink in concert and spend the night in the city with a group of girlfriends; I struggled to keep up with everything and didn't feel like partying. I just wanted to curl up in a bed. That huge difference in my normal energy was even noticeable to my friends. As I sipped my drink, my body began to ache and set off mild sharp pains through my chest.

I felt tired and nauseated by the cough that wouldn't let up. Something definitely wasn't right, and for other people to notice it, I knew I needed to do something. Maybe I was getting the flu. Maybe I needed antibiotics.

After that weekend, I went to a different doctor.

I mentioned the 'pulling' sensation and told him that I'd had it for the past five months. He reassured me like my other doctor that everything was fine, and diagnosed the symptoms as the typical after effects of mastitis. It didn't make sense. How could it still be an after effect after all this time? The sinking feeling in the pit of my stomach returned.

I was given penicillin for the flu, and told to go home and rest. Looking forward to recovering and having a normal conversation again without all the coughing, I convinced myself that I'd be fine.

Slight body aches began two days into taking the penicillin, resembling the aches at the onset of flu. I thought nothing of it until the following day when the aches became stronger. I couldn't understand why I was getting these aches two days into taking the medication. Shouldn't I be feeling better? The aches and pains started to worsen but thinking they were another side effect, I kept taking the medication.

By day four I couldn't move without being thrown into bouts of excruciating pain. The slightest movement would knock me down in agony. I'd find myself screaming, as if I were being beaten and tortured inside my body, as if all the muscles in my chest and the upper half of my back were being ripped out from under my skin! The pain would rip through my arms down to my fingertips, and would go on for hours.

I tried all types of over the counter pain relief we had at home and nothing worked. When the onslaught of pain stopped for a few minutes, I was left breathless and sweating with my heart racing and pounding in my ears. I thought it had to be an allergic reaction to the penicillin, so I stopped taking it.

Through the agony I struggled to move, let alone walk. I had no choice but to keep being a mum and keep moving. I started overdosing on pain relief, taking anything I could get my hands on, but nothing relieved it. I pictured some rare disease eating away at my muscles. *What's wrong with me?*

Collecting the kids from school one afternoon, I couldn't walk without hunching over and hugging my chest and rubbing my arms. It was pure torture. When I'd try to straighten my body, the pain would stab into me like a thousand knives digging into the middle of my back. Something was undeniably wrong.

Wanting a third opinion, I went to see a different doctor again, explaining to him in great detail the excruciating pain that had been consuming my body in the past week. I made him aware of every symptom.

'It sounds like the after affects of the viral infection you had last week. Sometimes bacterial or viral infections can affect the muscles. It should go away within the next few days or so. I'd like you to get a blood test just to confirm that everything is fine, but I'm sure it will come back clear. You'll be fine,' he explained.

'Should I have an X-ray just in case? Because it feels like it might be a pulled muscle or a pinched nerve. Or maybe there's a blockage somewhere,' I suggested.

'No, it's really not necessary. You'll be fine. I'm one hundred per cent certain that it's the virus that has gone to the muscles,' he reassured me.

He prescribed asthma preventers and inhalers for the cough, and Celebrex, a strong pain relief that I could take for the next two weeks. I was so relieved. Pain relief! Good, strong, pain relief! This medication was going to free me.

Shaking from the severity of the rupturing pain in my back and chest, I slowly crawled into my car and took a tablet, thinking that it would be an end to my suffering. Half an hour later the pain had almost disappeared. I loved this pain relief. No more grabbing and rubbing my arms in desperation. No more screaming and rolling around in agony. The pain was gone. Completely gone.

2

TRUST YOUR INSTINCTS

A whole week passed and, incredibly, I'd forgotten about the pain. I was entirely numbed from the medication. Totally alleviated and at ease. I must have imagined and exaggerated the whole thing. The dry cough that nothing seemed to fix was still apparent, but as long as I wasn't in any pain, I didn't care about it. I trusted the doctor's diagnosis.

Even when my voice changed, it didn't bother me. With each passing day, I sounded like a pubescent chipmunk, and assumed it was due to the constant coughing. At least my kids thought it was funny. My daughters begged me not to lose my 'new' voice. I wasn't exactly amused, but it was nice to laugh, even if it was at my own expense.

It was at a wedding reception some days later that I was plunged back into reality. While offering a blessing to the bride and groom with a small mouthful of champagne, the pain ripped through the Celebrex that I'd taken only a couple of hours earlier. I collapsed across the table, doubled over from the pain stabbing and ploughing through to my spine as it had days before. I grabbed my chest as my heart rate accelerated and held my breath.

'Paul, I need my tablets, *now*'! I screamed through clenched teeth. He ran out to the car while I stayed hunched over, not moving, scared to breathe. With every inhalation, the pain would plunge deeper into my chest and down my arm, with my muscles ripping at my skin. I half expected to see them bulge out of my arm.

Paul ran back with the tablets, handing me a glass of water and putting the tablets in my mouth, because I couldn't move. He brought the water to my lips and I furiously swallowed. I lay with my chest on the table as I waited for the pain relief to absorb into my bloodstream.

Oh, the relief was sweet.

The next day, I became tired. Really tired. Looking back over the past week, I started questioning myself. That pain was real. I couldn't have imagined it.

What if there *is* something causing these symptoms? Why did the pain attack when I consumed alcohol? What if the doctor was wrong? He's treating the pain, but what's causing it? Shouldn't we be investigating it with tests and examinations to start narrowing things down? Nothing made any sense

With all these questions in my head, I started researching the pain I had felt in my muscles. I found all sorts of different diseases and disorders. I stumbled upon a couple of cancer sites, but quickly clicked out of them. As if I had cancer . . .

I read about fibromyalgia and related my symptoms to the description of pain. That's it! That's what it is! I have fibromyalgia!

I went back to visit the doctor, pretty damn proud of myself that I had found an answer. We started discussing the disorder and how it affects the muscles and causes pain in the body. As we kept talking about it, the doctor felt that it was not what I had and we were getting off track. Checking my blood test results, he informed me that I had an elevated white blood cell count, which confirmed the initial diagnosis: the after effects of a viral infection.

So that explained it, then. It also explained the other symptoms. I was to keep taking the pain relief for the rest of the week since it was working. According to him, I wouldn't need pain relief for much longer.

Even with his reassurance, I asked for an X-ray. I didn't want to appear as if I was begging, but I was close to it. I needed to see for myself that the inside of my chest was normal, or see the lingering infection in my lungs for myself. It felt crucial to have an X-ray. But he told me that it wasn't necessary, and I went home frustrated and disappointed. Back to square one.

The fatigue and weakness started almost as suddenly as everything else had. I'd been tired the past week or so, and at first I thought it was something to do with the flu or just being a busy mother. I was exhausted and run down, taking naps with my son.

The two-week mark for this pain medication was drawing closer. Seeing the last of the tablets in the box, I remembered the very real pain and panicked. What if the pain started again? What do I do? Then, as if answering my own questions, it started, very faintly. Taking the medication every four hours just didn't cut it anymore. They would wear off after three hours.

The following day they only worked for two hours. The pain started all over again, with an increased intensity in between the dosages. As I was not supposed to take more than the four hourly dosage, I tried taking other analgesics in between, but nothing worked.

This is ridiculous! The doctor said the pain would stop, but it was getting worse!

Alarmed, I went back to the doctor. Regardless of the situation, I became an expert at reassuring myself that I was fine. I reminded the doctor again about all of my symptoms and my worry that I was on the last two days of pain relief. I told him how the cough was now developing into uncontrollable fits, that the asthma inhalers and preventers every hour on the hour were not relieving the cough at all. I told him how the pulling sensation and pressure associated with it was becoming increasingly uncomfortable, that the struggle and difficulty taking deep breaths had me worried as I felt suffocated, and that the sudden bouts of fatigue were weighing me down.

He heard my cough and saw the pain I was in. With that, he told me that the asthma inhalers were safe to take whenever I required them, and prescribed an even stronger pain relief that I could go on taking for the next two years! Two years? But what about all of my other symptoms? I convinced myself that once the pain went, everything else would follow.

Well, I was happy with that, wasn't I? *Karina*! I screamed at myself (in my head), maybe it is nothing*! Stop worrying!* Just listen to the doctor and everything will work out. *Don't panic.* Think positive. Yes, arguing with myself in my head in public, I was going insane. I went straight to the pharmacy.

I didn't realise at the time how lucky I was that the pharmacist working that shift knew me well, as my family and I had been going to this clinic for years. She was about to fill the prescription when she asked, 'Karina, do you know what this medication is?'

'Um, it's some sort of pain relief, isn't it'? I asked.

'Well, yes, you can use it for pain, but it's more for people suffering from some form of depression or schizophrenia. You need to know . . . The main side effect of taking this is, well, suicide,' she explained.

I paled.

She handed me an information booklet on the medication. 'Before I give it to you, you can read about it and decide for yourself if you need it,' she told me.

'I appreciate that,' I said numbly.

I'm not depressed. I'm not schizophrenic. Am I? Is that what the doctor really thinks? That I'm making it all up in my head? Oh my god, I must be crazy. As if answering my own subconscious crap, a spasm of pain ripped through my chest and my back, taking my breath away. Well, I couldn't have imagined that!

I thanked the pharmacist, hurried off to my car and raced home. I needed a tablet, now!

Once I was minimally anesthetised again (they weren't working like they used to), I started reading the information booklet. Despite the physical torture from what was like the depths of hell, I did not like the sound of this medication. This tablet blocks the nerve receptors in the spinal cord from receiving any messages of pain felt by the body.

I felt sick. I didn't want anything messing with my brain, my nerves, my spinal cord, and whatever else this would mess with.

And why was there so much attention on the pain instead of the cause of it? What if I were to take this tablet for the next two years, and the real problem coming from inside my chest (or my back) worsened? I knew that all these things were not an after effect of any viral or bacterial infection, cough or no cough, increased white blood cells or not. There was something more to this. I needed a fourth opinion.

Calling the clinic immediately, I finally made an appointment with my regular doctor. He'd help me. And if anything, he would reassure me that the previous doctors' diagnoses were correct all along, and confirm that I was crazy and it was all in my head. That's what I needed: confirmation of something and some reassurance . . . of something.

Pain of any sort had never bothered me previously. Medication was usually the last thing I resorted to when I got headaches, and I was becoming a regular pill popper, relying on the next pill for a modicum of relief. The next day, I went and saw Dr Raj.

Once again, I delved into the whole situation from the last three weeks. The pain, the symptoms, and everything else I had been going through. Fortunately, I didn't have to repeat all of it. Most of the information was already in my records because I was in the same clinic. Once I'd finished explaining, he looked concerned.

He was listening.

I asked him for an X-ray and when he agreed, I let out a pent-up breath of relief.

He filled out the referral form for me to go in as soon as they had an available appointment! Oh my god! I could have skipped out of the clinic, I was so excited! Before I left, he mentioned that if they found anything on the X-ray, he would ring me immediately the following morning, just to put me at ease, and we could then investigate further through other tests.

Awesome! And he extended the prescription of Celebrex for me—not the schizophrenic one. Brilliant!

I jumped into my car and called the MRI clinic immediately. I made the appointment and drove there straight away.

Getting the X-ray was easy. So why did I have to go through three weeks of pain, uncertainty and pleading, when an X-ray takes two minutes?

I was glad to finally have a window to the inside of my chest, and be able to see the reality of what was going on. Then I'd find out how to fix it.

The next morning started like every other morning. I'd taken the girls to school and put Jaivan down for his nap when I remembered the X-ray. No news is good news, I thought, until the phone rang. Crap.

'Karina, it's Dr Raj. It's about your X-ray. I need to see you. It's urgent. You don't need to make an appointment, just come in and I'll see you right away. You won't need to wait.' He sounded serious.

'OK, I'll come down now; is everything all right?'

'It's better if I speak with you here. Can you come now?'

'Yes. I'll leave now.'

The sinking feeling returned. No. I'll be fine. I had an answer and that's what I'd wanted.

My father came into the kitchen then, asking me who had called. When I told him the doctor wanted to see me, he looked just as panicked as I felt. Calming him down, I planted a semi smile on my face, and told him not to worry—it was probably procedure to speak with patients face to face rather than over the phone. I'd be home soon and it would all be fine.

I didn't believe a word coming out of my mouth.

In the car I nervously called my mum, telling her what the doctor had said over the phone and how insistent he was to see me. Mum reassured me not to worry, that it was probably some sort of an infection. Then why was I so nervous? Shaking my head, I laughed at myself. I didn't even know what was about to happen. 'Think positive,' I thought.

Arriving at the clinic, Dr Raj was waiting for me at reception. 'Don't panic. Just keep smiling and keep breathing,' I told myself under my breath. 'What ever it is, you'll fix it,' and I knew I would, no matter what. Since when had I ever given up on anything?

I didn't back down when I was bashed at the age of fifteen. I didn't back down when I was repeatedly molested during my childhood. And I certainly didn't give up when I was raped at nineteen. I kept going, kept living, used to dealing with the adversities of life. Being an only child, I had learnt to rely on myself. Compared to my past, this was nothing,

In Dr Raj's room, I saw his expression, his frown. He looked disappointed and sombre. I could see whatever he had to tell me wasn't exactly the best of news. Even though I wanted to find out what was wrong, I was secretly wishing there was a hole I could crawl into. Biting my lip to stop it from trembling, I patiently waited for him to start talking. I knew what was coming was bad.

Don't cry, Karina. Don't cry.

Clearing his throat, he began. 'Karina, they found a mass in your chest, so they're requesting you back for a CT scan to confirm what it is,' he told me, and reached for a referral form.

'What? What mass?' I asked.

He cleared his throat and stopped what he was doing. 'They found a tumour in your chest. It's approximately

8.6 cm long by 5.3 cm width, and seems to be sitting on top of your heart. Here, in this part of your chest,' he said slowly, pointing to the upper left side of his chest. 'It's displacing your trachea towards the right, which could explain the persistent coughing. You need to go in now for another scan to further investigate what it is, and then you will possibly need to see a specialist.'

Tears began forming in my eyes as I tried processing what he'd just said. Tumour? Did he say a tumour? I felt sick all of a sudden, as I tried swallowing the dry ball in my throat.

'Um, what do you mean by a tumour'? I asked, confused.

'At this stage, we don't know what it is, so you need to go in for a scan, and we'll take it from there,' he said.

'Dr Raj . . . isn't a tumour, cancer?'

'They're not sure what it is at this stage. You need another scan to confirm. We'll wait for the results of the scan before we can conclude anything,' he repeated gently.

He read the X-ray result to me, but it might as well have been in another language. I couldn't make sense of it. I couldn't hear him clearly, just a murmuring of words. My own thoughts were racing around trying to grasp what he'd just said. My head started spinning while my chair was slowly sinking into the floor as I felt a coldness wash over me. I froze. Nothing made sense. I heard somewhere the words thymoma and lymphoma, but what did that mean? Tuberculosis was mentioned in there too. Well, that's just stupid. Isn't it?

The sudden realisation of the word 'tumour' hit me hard. 'Dr Raj, am I going to die?' I asked, wiping away the beginning of tears.

He didn't answer me, reassuring me that this was why they needed a CT scan.

'I'll make the appointment now for you for a scan, and I'll see you again tomorrow for the results. One more thing: don't go and search anything on the internet. It's full of nonsense and will just scare you. You don't need to see that.'

Scare me? A mixture of adrenalin and nervousness pierced my heart. I got up slowly, smiled and thanked him for sending me to the X-ray, and numbly traipsed out to my car.

Driving to the MRI clinic, I phoned Mel, a good friend of mine who was waiting for my phone call about the results. Mel and our group of friends who had watched me disintegrate slowly over the previous weeks since the concert, were just as worried about it as I was.

As soon as I heard her voice, I broke down crying, confused as to what I was getting into and needing reassurance that I was going to be fine. I didn't know how to tell anyone else, and I couldn't bring myself to tell my family.

Arriving at the MRI nervous and scared, I looked around wondering what the other patients were facing. After changing into a gown, I was taken into the scan room. The machine looked huge and intimidating in the cold and dimmed room. The technician asked all the standard questions about allergies, if I suffered from claustrophobia, if I was on medication. The typical questions associated with a scan like this.

Our conversation led to my symptoms and what I had been going through for the last three weeks. She was surprised that it had taken this long to get to this point, but I just wanted answers.

She explained how the scan worked and that she had to inject the contrast dye through a vein in my hand. I agreed to the procedure and signed the form. In that moment I would have agreed to anything.

Then she explained that the iodine dye (aka contrast material) was to be used to make structures, or in my case, the tumour, easier to see on the CT pictures by lighting them up. The dye is also used to check blood flow, find any other tumours, and so on. As much as that word was terrifying me, I wanted to know if there were any of these masses anywhere else.

She warned me that the dye could cause some side effects such as itching, a feeling of warmth, the sensation of needing to pee, and a metal taste in the mouth, but that these sensations would only last a few seconds.

While lying on the table waiting for the scan to start, all I could think about was the conversation I just had with my doctor. I swallowed hard and could feel the pressure against my throat stronger than before. My heart began racing. My head began pounding. A tumour? This can't be happening!

The scan machine roared to life and it was so *loud*. The lights in the tube started circling around it. I panicked as the table I was lying on started moving, drawing me closer into the tube. Completely paralysed in my fear, I grabbed the blanket I was lying on and took all my anger out on whatever piece I was holding, clenching my fists in my rage. I didn't want to go through with this, with *any* of this. *What the hell am I doing here?*

I wanted to get out of there! To disappear! Trembling from an attack of nerves, right then, I knew in my heart that this was just the beginning. I knew there was more to come and that shocked me to my core. Silently crying, I couldn't stop my tears flowing down the sides of my face. I was terrified.

The technician stayed in contact with me the whole time through the speakers in the tube. She let me know when the dye was going to start running through my veins. Honestly, I didn't need the warning; the sensation was strong enough. When I started to feel the rush of warmth with the intense need to pee, my anxiety peaked and my heart raced faster.

Oh my god, *please* don't let me pee!

Ignoring that sensation, everything I had been through over the last few weeks started to hit me, and my tears fell faster. I looked at the machine as if it was my enemy. It was going to show me something I knew I didn't want to see. It's one thing wanting answers, but it's another to get answers you don't really want to hear.

I had the strongest urge to rip the needle out of my hand, jump off the table and run. Run far away from everything! Maybe I could disappear from this tumour, somehow escape it. But how? A tumour? Fuck!

The way my doctor evaded my questions, especially when I asked if it was cancer, really bothered me. I felt hot all of a sudden, as sweat mixed in with my tears. With so much adrenaline pumping through my body my mouth went dry.

I was incredibly relieved when the scan was over, and the effects of the dye had worn off.

Sitting anxiously in the waiting room, I saw the other patients through different eyes. I wondered if those people had just been given similar bad news. So many thoughts with way too much time on my hands. Just waiting.

Waiting was to become a huge part of my journey, but I didn't know that yet. I started hoping it wasn't a tumour, still not exactly sure what a tumour was. Tuberculosis sounded like a really good option. That could be fixed easily, right?

However, my instincts were telling me I already knew the answer. Not unlike past experiences in my life, another battle was about to unfold.

3

YOUR TEARS SHOW YOUR GREATEST COURAGE

Even though I lived only ten minutes away from the MRI clinic, the drive home seemed to go on forever. I had spoken to my mum on the phone and she was desperately holding onto the possibility that the X-ray images were a mistake. As I was saying the word 'tumour' to her, I couldn't help but break down and cry.

Through the uncertainty and confusion, it was too easy to jump to conclusions. We were hoping that the tumour was something that could be easily removed and we held onto that faith. I told her that if it turned out to be cancer, I'd fix it. I'd fight it with all I had. Both of us were gripping shreds of hope.

I had to call my husband, Paul, but I didn't know how to tell him. Steadying my voice, I said softly, 'Paul, the doctor rang me this morning about the X-ray results. They think there's a tumour in my chest, which would explain all the pain and symptoms I've been having.'

'What does that mean?' he asked.

'Well, I just went and had a CT scan which will hopefully confirm what it is,' I replied. 'The doctor said something like thymoma or lymphoma.' I didn't bother with tuberculosis.

'What's that?' he asked.

'I don't know. I think they're cancer, but I'm not sure. Dr Raj looked worried, Paul, and that worries me. He told me whatever I'd find on the internet would freak me out, so I'm going to look it up now. I need to know what I'm facing and he wouldn't really tell me anything. Paul, I'm scared.' I held my breath to stop myself from crying again.

He went quiet. I knew he didn't take it too well and it was hard for me to hear him like that, so I said a fast goodbye before quickly hanging up. I didn't want to waste any more time upsetting myself and everyone else, when it was probably nothing serious.

With the report in my hands, I typed in thymoma, since this was what the tumour was most likely to be, and the first word that I read was cancer. Of the thymus. Getting over that initial shock, I continued to read as much as I could understand, while trying to keep in mind that this was just a possibility.

There are so many websites packed with medical information, and the symptoms I was reading about started to add up. I had most of them: the persistent dry cough, shortness of breath, muscle weakness, upper body pain and aches, fatigue, dizziness, and a change in voice.

These symptoms are caused by the bulk of the mass pressing on the other major structures in the chest. Well, that made sense. Relieved to read that my symptoms were a normal part of the tumour, as unbelievable as that sounds, I kept reading. I wanted to know everything I could. I stared at the word 'cancer' for so long, it became a blur. OK, enough. How do I fix it? I looked up the treatment and found surgery. That gets rid of it! No big deal. I can do that! I would do it today if they'd let me!

I went on to research lymphoma, and there it was again: cancer—of the lymphatic system. This one had two types, Hodgkin and Non-Hodgkin, and within these types were more types, and again all of my symptoms added up. But there were also a few symptoms I hadn't developed: chills, night sweats, fevers, unexplained weight loss (I wish), appetite loss and itchy skin.

Well, it couldn't be lymphoma. The treatment? Chemotherapy for six months followed by radiation therapy, and no surgery unless for a biopsy. Oh no, then it definitely wasn't lymphoma. Remembering the documentaries I'd seen the year before about chemotherapy, my stomach turned. I didn't want to go through chemo. I didn't want to go down that road.

So it must be thymoma! Surgery and I'd be fixed in no time. No more pain. No more symptoms! They can just go in and take it out! I had to keep reminding myself that I had to wait for the scan results. Keep it real, I thought, just in case. But I couldn't contain my excitement. I wanted to call the doctor and reassure him I'd be fine. Ha! Reassure him, or reassure myself?

My father walked into the room and asked me what I'd found. For a second I forgot I was talking about cancer. I just began explaining all the information I'd read like I was talking about a common cold, like it was nothing. The initial shock of the X-ray result had worn off, replaced with sincere hope and excitement that I'd be better and back to normal in no time.

It wasn't real to me yet. There was no emotion connected to any part of it.

When I saw my poor father's face, I realised how matter-of-factly I was talking. He was finding it hard to take in, just as I had hours before. Sitting down in front of me, as white as his tanned skin would allow, he asked me to repeat everything I had just said. So I did, with a bit more care. I had to reassure him I'd be fine and that there was nothing to worry about. 'They don't even know what it is yet, so it might even be something else,' I said, trying to soften the blow. I definitely needed to learn to be gentler when talking about this to other people.

Dinner that night with the family was quiet—all caught up in our own agitated thoughts. No one was in the mood to talk or joke around. We didn't know what to talk about or how to start the conversation. They weren't sure if I *wanted* talk about it, and I didn't know if they were *ready* to talk about it. Mentally, we were all too busy. I didn't feel conscious, as if I wasn't in my body. I was sitting in a fog.

Losing my patience with the silence, I broke the ice. I put a movie on to distract the kids, and began explaining what I had read on the internet—the good with the bad. They had so many questions that I couldn't answer, so Google became my new friend. We all jumped online and started reading.

I had already made the decision to talk openly about it in front of my kids, keeping the traumatic stories from them of course. They didn't need to know about the deaths and fatalities associated with cancer. Just that it was a serious disease, like a bad case of chicken pox on the inside. They are a huge part of my life and I couldn't lie to them about having cancer.

Once everyone had gone to bed I started reading different articles on my own. Somewhere in the information about thymoma, I read an article about a girl who had passed away in her sleep. She was only eighteen. By this stage I had read many stories about people that had become victims to this awful disease, but this girl affected me. Why? Because her tumour happened to be in the same place as mine, sitting on top of her heart like mine, and roughly the same size as mine.

In the autopsy, it was revealed that the weight of the tumour was the cause of her death. It was too heavy for her heart to support it and it stopped beating. She had been getting the same symptoms as me for six months, going back and forth to the doctor asking for X-rays, and nothing had been done. This was one death out of many that could've been avoided.

Investigating other similar cases, it started to amaze me how many patients would be sent home time and time again from visiting their local doctor. Some had sought third and fourth, even fifth opinions, as I had. Some were even sent home after numerous hospital visits, taking up to a year to be heard. Some even longer than that. This infuriated me! Why is it, when cancer is one of the major killers in the world, signs and symptoms are continually overlooked and dismissed?

Too many doctors out there don't take their patients seriously. If someone has been suffering over a long period, why brush them off?

Going to bed that night, I couldn't sleep. I worried that my heart would stop beating from the weight of my tumour, so I stayed on my left side, too scared to sleep on my back. That's an awful way to go to sleep. When I finally did sleep, I'd wake up every hour in pain with my thoughts racing around until my head hurt.

The pressure of the tumour against my throat was always there, it was just hard to believe there was something inside me. I wanted to claw it out myself! How could this thing invade my body! I didn't give it permission! And why the hell did my body allow it?

Going through all the usual monotony the next morning, my mind was on another planet. The past three weeks and everything up until this point was like a bad dream I couldn't wake up from. Breakfast with a pill, lunch with a pill, dinner with a pill, not to mention all the paracetamol in between, like snacks. And pain ripping through my body, waking me up every night.

I didn't like living this way. I felt like a junkie needing a fix, but my fix was relief. I continuously felt the pain now; it was always with me, a constant reminder of what was growing inside of me. I couldn't switch my brain off, thinking, thinking, thinking. I was so glad that I had researched as much as I could. At least I would understand what was being said in future appointments. Well, I'd try.

I started to feel the reality of the situation, and it was overwhelming to say the least. I had so many answers to find out, yet I was nervous about the scan results, and knowing what I was dealing with and what the next step would be. My mum was coming with me, thank god.

On our way to the clinic, we were both trying our best to be positive and strong for each other, even through the peak of our anxiety. For the first time, no music played in the car. I couldn't concentrate. The thoughts in my head were loud enough.

When we arrived, I looked straight into my mum's eyes and held her hand. 'This is it,' I smiled to her.

'Yep, Karina, this is it.' Anxiety faded, and relief mixed with excitement took over.

'I don't want anyone to sugar coat it, Mum, I just want the truth.'

We were in the waiting room when Daniela, a nurse that knew me well from my previous visits, came by and asked me how I was doing.

'Not too good,' was my answer and, with that, tears welled in my eyes. Why the hell was I crying now? I was excited just two seconds ago! I must be going out of my mind.

Daniela quickly escorted us into an empty private room, and I told her everything. It was a huge release to talk to someone outside of my family, to get to this point. Being the beautiful person I would soon get to know, she cried with us and pulled me into a warm embrace, allowing me to cry on her shoulder. As a mother with two young children, she easily related to me and put herself in my shoes.

Some time went by and she had to see other patients. My mum and I nervously waited in the room, drying our stubborn tears. When the door opened and I saw Dr Raj, my stomach flipped. Here we go. You know those blood-curdling rides at theme parks, when you're clunking slowly up the tracks with your heart in your mouth, in a tiny little car, towards a giant drop. You pray your seatbelt stays secure and you don't fall out, and you're left hanging at the top at the point of no return. Well, I was on the edge and I was about to drop.

He sat down and clasped his hands on the table. He couldn't look at me for what seemed like a very long time. Everything was going in slow motion.

'Karina, the results are not here yet. I have been trying to call the radiologist all morning, but they're not there. Only the technicians are there today. I'm going to try to ask the radiologist working there tonight to send us the results tomorrow morning. But, because tomorrow is Saturday, there is no guarantee of getting the results until Monday. I'm sorry, Karina. I will try my best for tomorrow, but that's all I can do from this end.'

What? How was I going to wait three more days with no answers? I couldn't! Mum and I didn't say anything. Our mouths were clamped shut. Stupefied into semiconsciousness, I felt sick. But it was out of my hands and that realisation pissed me off. I don't like to rely on anyone for anything.

I found my helium voice and said to the doctor, 'But I don't know anything. I need to know what I have!'

He couldn't answer me. The amount of sympathy in his eyes was palpable, and my respect for him tripled.

These were not doctor-to-patient moments anymore. They were fast becoming more like two people sitting in a room, talking about the situation with care, respect and appreciation for each other as people. He didn't rush me through it, or throw me out. We were on the same wavelength and despite his busy schedule, he made the time to console me. He was just as concerned and disheartened as we were.

The room went quiet as we all processed having no results.

After a while, I couldn't stand the silence anymore. I needed some answers. Anything.

'I know that thymoma and lymphoma are both cancers, Dr Raj,' I whispered, with a guilty conscience. 'I looked it up.'

He cleared his throat. 'Yes, Karina, they are,' he said.

There went my stomach again, tied up in knots, gripping all of my insides and churning them in a whirlpool of trepidation.

'Karina, we just have to wait now to confirm. Come back early tomorrow morning in case the results come in. If they come in today I'll call you straight away. They are probably waiting for a second opinion to be sure, before they send us anything.'

Pushing all anger aside, I sympathised with him. I knew this wasn't his fault. I knew he'd been trying everything in his power to get answers for us, but unfortunately his hands were tied.

Although we were all deflated and filled with painful disappointment, I felt so grateful to have him as my doctor.

Mum and I drove home in silence. I stared out the window and felt a sudden envious resentment towards the people in the cars next to us. In that moment I would have preferred anyone else's problems to mine. I wished I could rewind the last few weeks, and go back to how life was before all of this started. I wished none of this were happening.

As confronting as it was, I Googled thymoma and lymphoma again and saw the very real images and photos of actual tumours. I could not believe that's what was sitting inside my chest, on top of my heart, and I could do nothing about it. All I could do was look forward to the next morning.

Later that night, I went to sleep, again on my left side, to help my heart keep beating. (I had to feel like I was doing something to help.) I could feel the heaviness of the tumour now. I felt the pressure of it, like someone was sitting on my chest, and when I moved onto my side,

I felt the tumour move with me, almost like falling to that side. I didn't know whether to laugh, scream or throw up.

I left early the next morning to see Dr Raj and he took me into the room straight away to let me know that no results had come in. He'd tried calling the MRI, but no one was working over the weekend. He felt terrible and didn't know what else to say. All we could do was wait for Monday morning.

The weekend passed by slowly. My kids were a wonderful distraction and my salvation. They helped us all forget about the seriousness of the situation. Any loud noise other than my own thoughts was comforting, and I was too tired to think any more.

We spent both days together in the same living room. This major life change we were all stepping into had shaken up the world as we knew it. A shift in our family began gradually, bringing us closer together, especially with Paul and me. Every moment he had, he would draw me into his arms and hold me. It was the safest place in the world.

Although I was anticipating the scan results Monday morning, I was dreading them at the same time. I knew I'd hear the word that I didn't want to hear, and wasn't ready to face.

Monday finally rolled around and Paul had decided to take the day off from work to go in with me. It was a relief to have him by my side offering his support. I was about to find out the truth of my health, and my fate, and I was a nervous wreck. My insides were mercilessly twisting and trembling again.

As we walked in to the clinic, my legs felt weak. I wasn't looking forward to what was coming. Looking at Dr Raj, I could tell he was just as nervous as us, and that was extremely humbling. He looked at my file, and told us that the results weren't in yet. Surprise, surprise. I became immune to those words, but it didn't stop the eagerness creeping up on me. My destiny was about to be revealed. I could feel it.

He picked up the phone and called the MRI clinic.

4

ONE DAY AT A TIME

The results came through the system almost immediately. Smiling, I couldn't wait to hear what they had found. Dr Raj read through them quietly to himself first.

When he was done, he printed them out and handed them over to me to read. But I had no idea what I was reading. The words were blurring into one big mess of ink. The connection from my eyes to my brain had decided to stop functioning.

I gave him the report back and asked him to read it to me.

'Karina, they are confirming the size of the tumour as the same size from the X-ray result, with another smaller lesion visible on the left lung the size of a fifty cent piece. That one is 3 cm by 3 cm. It's the lung that the mass is

touching. Because of its size, it's pushing and lifting that lung upwards, and pushing your trachea to the right.'

He went quiet, lifting his glasses and rubbing his eyes. 'Karina, they have advised further testing. You need a biopsy to confirm what it is. I think you should go to the hospital, right now. I will write you a referral letter and explain the situation to them so they can see you immediately.'

'Dr Raj, what do they think it is?'

'They confirm that it looks like a cancerous tumour, most likely thymoma because of the position it's in, but it's possible that it could be lymphoma. They mention tuberculosis as a precaution, but it looks more like a malignant tumour.' He looked at me with concern.

'It's OK Dr Raj, I'll be fine,' I said, apprehensively smiling, while swallowing back the tears that were threatening to break through my facade.

Trying to believe my own words, I looked over at Paul, expecting him to be fine. He was always so much better than me at holding it together and being strong, but his fear overpowered him. 'It's going to be OK, baby,' I reassured him. 'Don't worry. I'll be fine.'

Biting his lip, he grabbed my hand and held onto it, fearfully staring into my eyes for the longest time until I could see his own tears start to form.

I choked as I watched his despair, wiping away at my own frantic tears that had begun falling silently and uncontrollably.

Through the heartbreak of this truth, I felt strong and unstoppable as I stared at my hands in my lap. I told myself I could get through this. I needed to stay strong for my own sake.

Dr Raj handed me the letter of referral. All of my symptoms were listed on it. He detailed everything in that letter and gave me all of my blood test results and scan results. I wanted to hug him for helping me get this far. I couldn't help but think, what if I had listened to the other doctor and taken those 'suicidal' painkillers . . . for two years? The tumour would have kept growing and spreading. Shit. I read that the bigger they grow, the more aggressive they get. And with two tumours, it would have surely slowly killed me, whatever type of cancer this was.

On our way out of his office, Dr Raj handed me his card with his mobile number on it. He asked me to call his private number if I needed any further help. If it hadn't been for him listening to my desperation for an X-ray, and taking as much time as he could searching and explaining things to us, where would I be now?

We drove straight to the hospital in silence, both of us having too much to think about. I looked over at Paul, reached out for his hand, and didn't let go. For the most part, a big piece of me contained pure and honest to God relief that I was doing something. I couldn't wait to feel normal again, and having my life back to normal was the only hope I had to cling to.

We went straight to the emergency ward and I gave the referral letter to the nurse at reception. While she read it, I started explaining everything I had, all of my symptoms. I needed her to understand the desperation I felt.

She didn't care in the slightest. I kept trying, explaining the urgency of the situation and that I needed to see a doctor immediately, begging her for help. Nope. Not an iota of care. Imagine if it were happening to her, I thought, but getting angry wouldn't have helped.

So I waited and watched her discuss my situation with another nurse, so irritatingly calmly that I could have exploded. They suddenly looked at me with disgust, like I had leprosy, or worse. Wait a minute: last time I heard, cancer wasn't contagious! What the hell was their problem?

'Karina, we need to put you in confinement. We don't want to risk the health of anyone in this hospital.' Why? Is this how they treat cancer patients?

Seeing the confusion on my face, she continued. 'On your scan results, they've mentioned the possibility of TB, so we have to take all necessary precautions.' She'd cautiously taken a step away from me, and I couldn't help the rebellious snort that escaped from under my breath. Oh, it was going to be a long day.

She asked me a mountain of questions, tested my blood pressure, and escorted us to the 'confinement room.' Well, didn't I feel like a criminal.

So there we were, Paul and me, all by ourselves, locked in confinement. We looked at each other and cracked up laughing. The nurse came in and handed me a blue protective gown and mask like the ones the surgeons use during surgery. Only this mask was bright orange and shaped like a duck's bill. Oh, this just gets better, I thought.

She tried to persuade Paul to wear the 'duck bill' and blue gown, but Paul refused. He had a reputation he had to protect, and wasn't in the mood for dress-ups. And besides, we had lived every day together for the past nine years, with our three children, and none of them were sick. This mask thing was so unnecessary.

Wearing her blue gown and orange mask, the next nurse that came in perfectly resembled Donald Duck. She would be the one looking after me while we waited for the lung specialist. A lung specialist? Well, about time! Things were looking up! About six student nurses marched into the room in a straight line, also wearing the gowns and beaks. It was an incredible sight. If only we had filmed it.

Paul had to turn to face the wall to stop himself from laughing.

We exhaustedly waited all day, but the relief of being in hospital lifted a huge weight off my shoulders.

While we waited, the army of student nurses would come in every twenty minutes and ask me the same recurring questions. I found myself repeating the same things incessantly. It was clear to me they had no idea what they were doing and that was frustrating.

When the lung specialist finally came in, I could have hugged him. He announced to all the staff to take off their gowns. The party was over. This was a man on a mission.

He asked me an array of questions. Had I experienced unexplained weight loss? I wish. (He didn't laugh.) Was I suffering from chills and night sweats? No, and no. Did

I have itchy skin? No. I couldn't help but think maybe I should be saying yes, just to speed things up.

He explained to me that the tumour definitely looked cancerous and studying the scan images and judging by all of my symptoms, he was sure it was thymoma. He explained the procedures of surgery to us, that it was a matter of going in and removing the tumour. After that, a six-week recovery period would follow, and all's well that ends well.

A wide smile spread across my face.

The size of the tumour alarmed him and he disappeared as quickly as he had come in. After a while a cardiothoracic surgeon came in. She introduced herself so quickly I didn't catch her name. She immediately started talking about biopsies, and needles, and testing, and weeks followed by more weeks, and confirming results. There was no mention of surgery. Just a rush of words.

'So, when is my surgery?' I asked her.

'Oh, you won't be having surgery. I want you to come back in two weeks' time for an appointment about discussing a possible needle biopsy. I'll be talking to my team to get their views on what they think is the next best step for you and your case. After that consultation, you'll have to wait another week or two for the actual biopsy. From then, the results usually take about another two weeks,' she said.

All the blood drained from my face. The ground was swallowing me up again and everything went eerily quiet. All I could do was stare at her. I was trying to add up all those weeks she'd just said in my head. What happened to surgery?

She went on, 'Well, we need to confirm what the tumour is. We can't just cut you open without knowing what we're dealing with,' she said, exasperated, and very abruptly. Huh? Wait a minute . . . was she getting annoyed with me? Before I'd even opened my mouth?

'So I have to keep waiting for another two weeks, just to find out if the next step is a needle biopsy?' I asked numbly.

Then wait another week or two for the actual test, and then another two weeks after that for results? Five to six weeks! Is she insane?

'Look, you've waited this long, another two weeks isn't exactly going to make a difference,' she said sarcastically. I don't think I've ever met anyone in my life as cold as her.

'Can't I just be booked in for a biopsy from today?' I asked.

I understood completely about not having surgery without confirmation first. What I couldn't understand is why I had to wait so long, just to *discuss the possibility* of a needle biopsy. *I can't wait any more! Book me in now!* I screamed in my head.

'Look, Karina, go home. There's nothing more we can do for you here. I'll see you in two weeks and talk to you then. That's all I will do.' She was getting angry and impatient. But I didn't give a shit. No way!

The room was spinning again. With my heart in my mouth I tried to stay calm, and desperately began explaining all of my symptoms to her, but she cut me off.

'Yes, I've already read about you and your condition,' she said. My jaw dropped.

'But my pain medication doesn't work anymore!' I continued. I needed her to understand I was getting worse by the day! I was close to getting on my knees to beg her for mercy!

'What do I do about the pain when the pills stop working completely?' I asked.

'Look, I'll give you a prescription for Oxycontin, which is stronger morphine-like pain relief. You take one every six to eight hours. They will last you longer until I see you again, and are safer to take than the Celebrex you've been taking,' she explained. Well, that was the least she could do.

All I could do was stare at her, my mouth gaping. I felt like we were in reverse. I knew she had the authority to book something in that moment, or have the consultation while I was already in the hospital.

Why wouldn't she listen to me! Beyond frustrated, I wanted to *scream*!

And then, she said something to me with such a sarcastic smirk I swear I will never forget it. 'Look, Karina, you've obviously had this tumour growing in your chest for a while now. It's not like you're gonna die tomorrow.' She laughed, smirking at her own joke.

I looked over at Paul. His jaw had practically fallen to the floor. I wanted to slap the smugness off her face. She was infuriating! But I couldn't move. I couldn't even speak. All I could do was stare at her in disbelief.

And with that, I changed back into my clothes, and we left, dazed and in shock.

We couldn't believe the insensitive and blunt way she had treated us. We were just another number, like cattle waiting in line in a slaughterhouse.

Reading the appointment form that the surgeon had given me before I left, I shook my head. I just couldn't believe I had to keep waiting, when she could clearly see what I was going through. She had seen the scan and the tumour for herself. The size of it had worried the few doctors and specialist I'd seen already, but no, not her. 'She's not going to take me seriously, Paul,' I said. I hoped I could see someone else at this next appointment.

We drove straight to Dr Raj's clinic. He saw us immediately, excited to know what had happened. We explained it all and he couldn't believe what we were telling him. More to the point, he couldn't believe that she was making me wait so long for a consultation.

But there was nothing we could do. We had no choice. My life was in her hands now. I felt helpless and chained down—back to square one, *again*.

If anything happened to me during this whole waiting game, you could bet she'd be hearing from me. From all of us. And if I died? (Yes, the thought crossed my mind.) I'd be rattling some huge ass shackles and haunt her for the rest of her life.

On the way home, I had flashbacks of my dad's cancer scare. He is not a man that shows any type of pain or walks around telling people he's sick. My dad very much gets on with it. But this one particular morning he was screaming in agony, grabbing his stomach and keeling over in pain. I had never heard my dad scream before.

I drove him to a clinic where a doctor began poking and prodding his abdomen. While my dad screamed, this doctor tried to pick me up, as if we were in a sleazy bar. I was speechless at first, thinking it must have been in my head.

My dad noticed it, rolled off the table and we left, nicely suggesting he have his medical license reviewed. How do these people become doctors?

Five CT scans and six weeks later, they found a tumour in his kidney. But, if my dad had settled at the first, second, third and fourth diagnosis of kidney stones throughout those torturous six weeks he was in severe pain, who knows what would have happened.

The tumour had grown and spread through his entire kidney and the surrounding tissues. The way the doctors spoke to him when they finally confirmed his tumour was a huge blow and disgusted us back then. 'Oh, he has cancer, that's all. What did you expect?' Do these people know what feelings are? Are they human?

He was fine after they removed his kidney, but it took a huge emotional toll on him and on my mother and me.

So, the waiting game continued. At the very least, I knew there was something in my chest, and things had been set in motion. Sort of.

I knew I had to start telling people then because they had already seen my health plummet and were waiting on answers.

I spoke to Mel again and she could tell I wasn't in the best place to be talking to anyone else just yet, so she offered to talk to our other friends for me, like my personal spokeswoman. Mel is the human version of a loudspeaker.

It's not that I didn't care about anyone else, I just didn't have the energy to explain things over and over again. There would be a million questions I didn't have all the answers to, and it was still new and raw to me. I avoided going out of the house for a couple of days, secluding myself from the world. It wouldn't last long, though. I knew I had to face people eventually.

When I went to the school to pick up my kids I saw them. People all around me. Everywhere. I cringed. I was way out of my comfort zone. Breaking the news to family and friends would have to be one of the hardest parts of this whole experience.

I'd reached my friends, we said our hellos, and then awkward silence followed. Nobody knew what to say, whether to speak, or how to start. Where's a damn hole when you need one?

The ice was broken quickly. It just took one of them to ask me how I was feeling to start the conversation. Some cried from the shock of hearing 'cancer'. Some were sympathetic, hugging me straight away. Some were strong and behind me, angry at the tumour and the fact that I had to go through this. That was my favourite.

Dealing with people is how I learnt to become strong and optimistic. I found myself saying things like, 'It's fine, I'll be all right, don't worry about me.' Instead of people comforting me, I learnt quickly that I would be the one comforting them, and I was OK with that. I was like their support person.

I had a lot of good support around me, but with the good comes the bad. The nightmare stories started rolling in. These stories would come at me from everywhere, some from people I didn't really know. I would hear them from all directions.

'My sister had a cousin who knew a friend of a friend's husband that had something like lymphoma . . . and he died.' Just keep smiling and nodding, Karina.

'I knew a girl who was a friend of my boss's mum, and she had cancer and it keeps coming back, and she gets really sick and she looks like crap.' OK.

Probably the worst was, 'My girlfriend's aunty had breast cancer, and she had chemo. Chemo's shit. Don't tell me you have to go through chemo. Oh, you poor thing. If you do you're really going to suffer. You'll feel like shit. You'll *look* like shit! You'll be so sick, vomiting everywhere, all the time. Chemo is awful. You'll be in so much pain you'll *wish* you were dead.' On that note, seclusion, here I come!

I learnt how to power walk to and from my car with my kids like walking a marathon. I just wanted to hide. I didn't want to hear anymore. I preferred being under house arrest than hearing that.

Being newly diagnosed, I got tired of all of the commotion surrounding me very quickly. I just wanted to be treated like a normal person. I missed talking about things other than cancer. I didn't want to hear 'you poor thing' anymore. I became tired of hearing the same 'think positive' and 'be strong, you'll be fine,' when I was fine!

The last thing I wanted, or needed, was to be made into a victim, and to be looked at like I was already lying in a casket. I was still Karina 'the person' not Karina 'the disease'. Death was the last thing on my mind until people started putting it into my head.

I became extremely grateful for the few close friends I had. They would only ever ask me how I was feeling, and then have the usual conversations we'd normally have. They would talk to me about whatever was happening in their lives, all their dramas and problems.

All the single friends would talk about how much sex they were having, while all the married ones would be talking about how little sex they were having. The perfect conversations and distractions I needed to keep my mind off tumours and cancer.

I didn't have to hear any horror stories when I was with them. I didn't have to try to be strong, with 'think positive' being thrown in my face every five minutes. I was allowed to just be, and that's what I loved.

5

GET ANGRY

During the two weeks waiting for the discussion with Dr Stoneface Surgeon (her new name), my health started to deteriorate with new symptoms manifesting almost daily. The chills would attack suddenly and I would watch my lips and fingertips turn blue. My body would become like a block of ice, completely frozen. I might as well have been lying naked in the snow.

The shivering and trembling that came with it was uncontrollable. My teeth would chatter and my body would be covered in goosebumps. No amount of quilts or blankets, jackets or jumpers or hot water bottles would work to warm me up.

Along with the chills, the upper body aches and pains would start. I'd have to take Oxycontin to stop the pain, but the chills wouldn't stop. In my desperation, I would take paracetamol and jump into a hot shower. That worked.

I fast became my very own science experiment, trying anything until I'd find the solution.

My exhaustion would throw me into deep, short naps, at any hour, that were hard to wake up from. When I did wake up, I'd be sweating so much that I had to change my clothes.

When a few days had passed, the sweats would be ignited by scalding fevers inside my whole body. Although it was the middle of winter, I was sweltering, roasting from the inside in heat waves.

Every morning I would burst through the doors into my back yard and into the cold air, desperate for some relief from the scorching furnace my body had become. Is this what menopause felt like? I watched my mum go through it. She was pretty funny to watch, fiercely ripping her clothes off every time she boiled up.

Now I was doing it. I laughed at myself, while I ripped my clothes off, frantically waving my hands around to fan myself outside. It was usually around 6:00 in the morning and seven degrees celsius.

The lymphoma symptoms I had read about stirred in my memory. Could it be Lymphoma? No. Treatment for that was chemotherapy, remember? That's not going to happen to me.

The cough I had was becoming extremely annoying and frustrating. I couldn't talk at all without flying into coughing fits. I'd say one word, and cough. Another word, another cough. Even laughing became a chore. A mixture of laughing and coughing would end in a struggle to breathe.

I developed a laugh phobia and held my laugh when something was funny. As hard as it was, the fight to breathe afterwards wasn't worth it. This became my new way of life.

The pressure on the side of my throat was becoming severely uncomfortable. It felt like a relentless fist pushing down hard into my throat. I would dig my fingers into my neck and try to move the tumour over, just for some relief. Of course, that didn't work.

And my voice? Well, I was officially now a high-pitched, constipated sounding, high on helium, chipmunk. There was no hint any more of the voice that I had lived with my entire life. That was when I was able to speak. Mostly it would interchange. I would go from having a voice, to nothing but a whisper.

I had never really suffered from headaches before, but they started coming now. Strong, temple-thumping headaches, stemmed from the back of my head. When the effects of the morphine stopped, the headaches would start along with the excruciating upper body pains. I would run to the kitchen, and pop that tablet as if it was saving my life.

With all of these symptoms, I felt myself spiralling downhill and getting worse with each passing day.

The day before the looming consultation, I woke up alone in my own personal oven of heat and dripping sweat. It was 6:30 in the morning. Paul had already left for work and the kids were still sleeping. As I changed my clothes and cooled myself down in front of the fan, I was deep in thought.

I started worrying about Paul. I worried if something did happen to me, what would he do? How would he cope? Who would be there for him? As much as it hurt, I forced myself to think the worst.

Absentmindedly, I grabbed my phone and went to the toilet, locking the door behind me, before bursting into tears. I found myself crying against the wall, sliding down to the floor, asking myself the only question I wanted an answer to: why? Why was this happening?

I called Mel. She heard in my voice that something was wrong.

'Mel, I need you to promise me that if anything happens to me, you're going to be here for Paul and the kids. Please, you have to help him. He'll be completely lost if . . . you know . . . if anything happens to me. I don't think he'll be able to manage with the kids and deal with losing me, on his own.'

'Shut up, dude, don't be an idiot. Nothing's going to happen to you. Just wait and see what happens at the next appointment. Don't stress, mate. I know it's shit right now, because you're waiting for answers, but try not to freak yourself out. You're going to be fine, hon, you have to believe that. And whatever you face, you've got all of us girls going in with you, OK? You know that don't you?'

'Yeah, I know, thanks, Mel. But, still, just promise me,' I whispered through the torrent of tears streaming down my face.

I needed her to promise me that she would be there for him in his hardest moments. I trusted her, and I knew she would keep that promise. Cancer was no stranger to her, as her family has had to battle it many times, so she understood how I felt.

Still in the toilet once we'd hung up, I took advantage of the moment and let myself cry. And I cried hard, hitting the wall and asking nobody in particular, *'Why?'* With my head in my hands, the reality of what I was about to endure was beginning to hammer me.

I was unusually emotional, and I didn't understand it. 'I must be hormonal,' I thought. Maybe I'm getting my period. I pulled myself together, worried that my kids would wake up and catch me close to a nervous breakdown. I was on the verge of a very real meltdown.

After checking myself in the bathroom mirror and washing the tears from my face, I went to Aaliyah's room. I leaned in and watched her sleep, listening to her breathing. My first-born child. Was I going to see her grow into a beautiful woman? Was I going to be her best friend when she needed someone? A lump in my throat threatened to start the crying again, and I had to stop myself.

Walking over to Monique's room, I saw how peaceful she looked in her deep sleep. Listening to my baby's breathing was music to my ears. The tears flowed faster. I couldn't bear leaving them in the world. I longed to be there, beside them, for as long as life would allow me. I can't leave them. I have to do this, I thought. I have to do this for them.

It was difficult taking my girls to school that morning. I didn't want to leave them, and secretly wished I could keep them at home with me. I didn't want to be alone. I wanted my family around me, but I knew they needed the distraction of school and being with their friends.

It was like I was saying goodbye to them for the last time. Why, I don't know, but that's how I felt. I held on to them, squeezing them with all my strength, and they squeezed me back, letting me hold them for as long as I needed to. They needed to be held just as much as I did. Aaliyah wept quietly in my arms, whispering, 'I love you, Mama,' as we held onto each other. As much as I had kept the worst of cancer from them, she was old enough to understand what it meant.

I hugged her harder, kissing her on her forehead and telling her how much I loved her, holding onto my own tears. I kissed them both as many times as I could, loving them and loving that moment, needing that closeness and dreading letting them go. Finally, I walked them to the crossing and watched them walk away. It killed me to say goodbye.

When I got home, my father was sitting in his usual spot at the front of the house, staring out the living room windows, deep in thought. He looked me over, shook his head in disbelief, and continued staring out the window. Seeing me become so sick was hurting him beyond anything I could ever imagine.

I turned to my son, holding him close to me for as long as he'd let me. Once I put him down for his morning nap, I found myself staring at all of his features:

his tiny hands and fingers . . . his miniature nose . . . his small lips that were twitching from his dream. I caressed his cheeks, telling him how much I loved him, and then I burst into an uncontrollable fury of tears that I couldn't stop.

Looking up I screamed in a whisper, '*Why? Why is this happening?* He doesn't even know who I am! He doesn't know who his mother is! It's not *fair*! How is any of this *fair!*

Collapsing onto the floor, I grabbed my legs, crying into my knees. Being in that position, the pressure from the tumour against my throat was overwhelmingly constrictive, to the point of strangling me, but I didn't care. Seething with rage, I cried and screamed hysterically into my knees. Is this it? Am I going to die? I'm thirty years old! Is this really how it ends? My life as I knew it was crumbling around me.

All I could see were the vivid images of Paul and our girls in my head. Our wedding day surrounded by my family. My baby boy in my womb as we said our vows to each other, as we promised each other forever. Was I really going to break that promise now?

I cried harder as I pulled myself up and looked at my son. He was so peaceful, sleeping and dreaming. What a beautiful baby boy I had. What a beautiful family we had created. And what for? To be torn apart and broken? To be taken away from them? From me? No! NO! This can't be happening. This *has* to be a *dream*! How can *any* of this be *real*?

I was inconsolable. I bent over the cot, still looking at my son. I lost track of time as I thought about everything. My life. My parents. How would they cope with losing their daughter? It would kill them to watch me deteriorate. To watch cancer take my last breath.

Were my children really going to be left without a mother? Was I going to miss out on watching my children grow and celebrate their birthdays? See who they become when they're older. Who will be there to wipe their tears and catch them when they fall? *I* gave them life! *I'm* supposed to be beside them, every step of their lives! My tears fell in streams.

My hopes and dreams about being a part of their lives until we are all old and grey, holding them in my arms for as long as life would allow me. Were those dreams going to be shattered and taken away from all of us? Was I going to become just a faded memory?

No! I haven't had enough time with them! I can't go now! Not yet! I'm not finished!

Right then, I stopped as anger exploded in my blood and boiled in my gut. I quickly wiped my tears. I held my son's hand, making a promise that I hoped to god I could keep and knew in my heart that I would try with every ounce of faith I had. 'I will *not* leave you without a mother. I'm going to *fight*! *Fuck you, cancer*! I have too much to live for! You won't take me down without a fight. *Fuck you*'!

That was it. The love I have for my kids along with the thought of leaving them fired me up and pushed me to find the strength that I never knew existed within me. My will to live was awakened.

Not only had the reality of what I was about to go through finally hit me, but the horror death stories people would tell me began to have an effect on me. Cancer and death seemed to go hand in hand.

I promised myself at that moment to block them out, and take them for what they were . . . just stories. I had to stay away from negativity and concentrate on myself, my health and my family. I'm not going to die! Not yet, anyway, and the less I listened to people's bullshit, the better.

The next day, my mum came with me to the consultation. While we sat in the waiting room, I hoped I didn't have to face Dr Stoneface Surgeon again. I hoped my case had been given to someone else—when I saw her. Dread tied my stomach in knots.

I knew that if I had to go through her, she would make me wait till Doomsday to destroy this tumour.

As she stalked out of the room, I let out a sigh of relief. I was telling mum about her callous bedside manner when she appeared again. 'Oh, no no no, oh, no. Please don't call my name'! I grabbed my mum's hand as if I was five years old again. She called my name. Damn it.

She smiled. Or half smiled. Well, that was a positive. She walked us to her room, and sat down. She asked me how I was feeling. Honestly, that shocked me. 'Maybe she does care,' I thought. I started to explain to her that everything was getting worse with new symptoms appearing in the last two weeks.

As I spoke she cut me off. Aha! There she was again, completely uninterested in what I was saying. I looked over at my mum. It was her turn to drop her jaw to the floor, as mine and Paul's had weeks before. I would've laughed if I weren't so uncomfortable.

Dr Stoneface proudly announced to us that she had spoken to a team of doctors about my case, and that they had all come to an agreement. I had to wait two weeks for a CT guided needle biopsy to confirm what type of cancer the tumour was. Like I had to be grateful she was going to perform some sort of miracle. She went on to explain how the procedure is performed, but I blocked her out. I didn't want to hear her voice or see that sarcastic smirk anymore.

She warned us that the results could take two to three weeks to come back, but they'd most likely be inconclusive. Then we'd have to follow up with more consultations to discuss further 'possible' investigations and tests. She continued her version of half smiling. Was this fun for her?

She had all the forms and papers right in front of her and told us to fill them out. My mum couldn't believe what she was hearing. I had to wait another two weeks for an inconclusive test? Mum burst into tears. I hadn't seen her cry like that since, well, ever.

My mum is a strong woman. With all the hardness life has thrown at her, being abandoned as a baby, growing up on the streets of third world Colombia on her own, she knows only too well how to get on with life, how to 'suck it up' and keep moving forward. Out of everyone I know, my mum has every right to be a stone-faced bitch, but she is the exact opposite. She is a warm, compassionate, patient, caring and empathetic woman, the best friend, mother and grandmother anyone could ask for, always putting others before herself.

Mum had stayed strong in front of me since finding out about the tumour, but now she was furiously crying next to me, desperately begging the surgeon to stop and listen to all of my symptoms. Listen to her concerns that I was rapidly getting worse by the day. The surgeon was about to interrupt, but my mum kept talking over her. 'Karina is getting so sick! What if this was your sister, your mother, or your friend? Would you care? Would you do things differently? Please, help her. *Please!*'

Of course, it didn't work. I braced myself as tears sprang into my eyes. Oh great. I didn't want to cry. There was no point.

We were wasting our time and I couldn't be bothered hearing anymore. I stood up and grabbed my mum's hand to help her up and lead her out of the room. She was broken. The reality of what I was going through was hitting her, and the hardest thing to swallow was that we were being left in limbo, left to wait again, and nothing was being done. I've never seen her look so lost. I hugged her and held her tight as she cried on me, her tears soaking into my shoulder.

At the reception desk, I filled out all the necessary forms for the needle biopsy and collected another prescription for more Oxycontin. We were given the appointment form and we left.

6

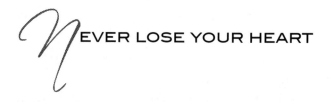

*N*EVER LOSE YOUR HEART

And so I waited. We all waited. I kept myself busy for those two weeks, reading books, watching cooking shows and fantasy movies—anything that could take me away on a journey far from the one I was on.

Since I had been too shocked to listen to the surgeon explaining the needle biopsy procedure, I had to research it on the net myself, but I couldn't understand the articles I found. I read paragraph after paragraph, with absolutely no idea what I'd just read. Why couldn't they just write in simple English with easy to understand descriptions?

I understood something about the doctor using a CT machine as a guide. I knew that machine well. I had a love/hate relationship with it since it had confirmed the tumour in my chest. The biopsy is done with a needle inserted into the chest and samples are taken from the tumour. Sounded simple enough. The more I read, the more excited I became.

The biopsy day finally rolled around, and I was happy to go on my own. My 'break from the world' time, I guess. But, Mel ended up taking me to the biopsy appointment. With her driving, she was likely to kill me before the tumour did.

We were in for a very interesting day, regardless of the situation.

I swear they could hear us laughing from the bottom of the hospital to the top floors. We were always loud . . . wherever we went. Restaurants, cafes, movies, funerals, it didn't matter.

When they called my name, we went serious. They wheeled me over to the ultrasound room on the trolley bed. Trolley bed? Well, Mel just about wet herself. When she stopped laughing at me, we tried to figure out why I was going to the ultrasound room instead of the CT room.

I felt like some sort of celebrity being driven around. When the staff would read my sheet about tumours and cancer, it amazed me how sweet, warm and sincere they'd become. People were at my service—even Mel became my personal assistant whom I would snap my fingers at to get me a cup of water.

I could definitely get used to this.

Once in the room, the doctor who would perform the biopsy explained that he wanted to try the procedure using the ultrasound machine first before trying it out with the CT machine. Even though it would be an easier way of doing it, he doubted it would work. Lying in my trolley bed, I had all the time in the world to try whatever he wanted.

When the images came up on the screen, no number of past ultrasounds could have ever prepared me for this. Our mood dropped and we became serious again. All we could see was black. The other structures in the chest were slightly visible, but ultimately everything was black. 'What's all the dark stuff?' Mel asked. I couldn't really ask anything. I was too fascinated by what was on the screen.

I knew it was the tumour before the doctor said it. But to see it for myself for the very first time was incredible. It's hard to accept that there really is something inside you that shouldn't be there, and there was always a part of me that was suspicious. The nagging thought that maybe this was all wrong. A misdiagnosis. A bad dream. But the blackness on the screen forced it onto me. It's true, it's in there, and it's real.

The technicians weren't happy with the visibility from the ultrasound. The image wasn't clear enough. It looked muddy. They wouldn't be able to perform a successful biopsy so I had to go into CT.

The assistants wheeled me into the hallway just outside of the CT room. Apparently I was due for the biopsy in ten minutes. I would soon learn that a hospitals version of ten minutes is more like an hour.

So we waited . . . and waited. Mel was tired of standing and jumped onto the trolley bed with me. We ripped out our iPods, and started our very own karaoke session in the middle of the hallway. Mel morphed into Pink and I was Janet Jackson. Well, we had to do something.

We must have been loud, grabbing the attention of everyone walking past us. In between fits of laughter at me sounding like I was singing on helium, Mel spoke to everyone passing by, asking the other patients how *they* were feeling, starting conversations at random. Completely distracted, I forgot what I was doing there.

After waiting the hospital's version of ten minutes, I was finally called in to the CT room. Being wheeled in, my stomach flipped. Here we go, I said to myself, taking a deep breath. They had already set the room up and were waiting for me. As I was transferred onto the CT table, I stared at my beloved enemy friend. Hello Mr CT. Every little thing I had to go through with it would bring me one step closer to the truth.

I nervously rubbed my frozen fingers, trying to hide the panic. It was weird. One minute I was smiling and laughing as Ms Jackson, the next I was trying hard not to fall into an emotional heap.

The doctor and technicians were prepared for anything in case something went wrong. What could go wrong? I wondered.

The doctor explained the procedure to me. I watched his mouth move, but I wasn't hearing a word of what he was saying. My ears had gone numb, deafening and drowning out the sound of his voice. I just kept smiling and nodding through my own private moment of insanity.

I heard something about using the CT images while the needle was being inserted into the tumour. He'd see the direction the needle was going, hopefully without damaging any other structures that were surrounding the tumour, like major blood vessels, nerves and so on. That put me at ease . . . sort of.

The nurse applied the antiseptic, and prepared me for the 'minor surgery,' as they had called it. She injected the anaesthetic through the chest tissues. Ow! 'Are you ready, Karina?' the doctor asked me. No. Yes. I don't know. My stomach was churning inside out. The anticipation of knowing the truth behind the tumour turned my answer into a 'Yes, I can do this.'

The CT machine had already been humming and turning through the doughnut shaped tube. The table started moving in towards the tube, and my tears began building up in my eyes. I swallowed back the tears, stopping them in their tracks, and sent out a silent prayer to God that nothing would go wrong. With the scan images coming through, the doctor began explaining his observations.

'Karina, the mass has wrapped itself around some blood vessels in your chest. It's going to be difficult, but I will try my best to get the sample you need. If you start to feel any dizziness, numbness, or if something generally doesn't feel right, please let us know.' I nodded. Oh god.

I was moved out of the tube as he watched the images that had been taken on the screen, and he inserted the biopsy needle. Thank god I couldn't feel it. It was huge. Facing the opposite direction of the screen I could only imagine what was happening. I moved into the tube again as more images were taken to see exactly where the needle was headed.

Once I was out of the tube, he pushed the needle deeper into my chest. I felt the pressure of it going in, but no pain. This went on for a while. In . . . then out . . . then back in again, until the needle was fully pierced into the tumour. I peeked at the image while he had his back turned. Fuck! It looked huge!

My heart sank.

Don't cry, Karina. Be strong.

I felt the clicks of the needle while he was getting the sample. This definitely was not a dream.

He recovered two more samples, and it was over.

The doctor asked me how I was feeling, and I felt fine . . . and a bit stupid for letting myself get caught up in so much anxiety. The blanket covering me was stained with a lot of blood and I hadn't felt a thing, no pain whatsoever. I had never had surgery in my life so I didn't know what to expect. I was a surgery virgin until that day. Ironically, it felt like I'd been invaded against my will.

They wheeled me back to the ward, and I realised I'd been in the CT room for close to two hours. Strange, because it didn't feel that long. Lying there staring at the ceiling on my own, my thoughts were racing again. I wished I had an off switch. I couldn't believe I had just seen my tumour, this horrible evil bastard thing that had a mind of its own, growing inside me. So much darkness taking over my chest. How bad is this thing? Is it growing faster now? My face went hot as rage erupted inside me. I couldn't wait to get rid of this shit.

Some time passed, and I started to feel drowsy as my nerves calmed down. The doctor came to see me to find out if I was feeling OK. In our conversation, he told me that the biopsy results would more than likely come back inconclusive, because the sample sizes are usually too small to get a positive result.

That's exactly what Dr Stoneface Surgeon had said, so why the hell was I having it done? Even *he* was surprised that I wasn't having a surgical biopsy instead, as they would need a much larger sample to test it. Concerned about the size of the tumour, he was afraid that the needle biopsy wouldn't be enough. He couldn't understand why we were wasting time. I should have been looking at proper surgery and treatment, instead of small sampled biopsies.

With his years of experience, he believed I had lymphoma. Well, shit. I made a mental note to go research lymphoma again. It pissed me off to know that the surgeon was playing with my life. Her words replayed in my head, 'It's not like you're going to die tomorrow.'

And the worst was that there was nothing I could do. Absolutely nothing.

Then, the excruciating pain that had been plaguing me from the very beginning slowly began breaking through the local anaesthetic. The doctor explained to me that it was inevitable because the tumour had been moved during the biopsy with all of the prodding and piercing, and it may have started pressing down on different structures in my chest. Perfect.

Suddenly, the pain came on intensely strong and fast, before I had a chance to catch my breath. Incredibly powerful assaults all over again. I hated that pain. It was all too familiar. I'd been able to live without it for so many weeks, avoiding it with all the medication, and now it was back, seeking revenge with attacks worse than I remembered.

Rolling around the bed, rubbing my arms and chest, I was desperate for it to end. Brutal flames erupted through my chest, down my arms and all across my back, more violent than before. A huge knife stabbing me over and over through my spine, ripping into all of my tissues and muscles without remorse. I screamed through the agony, as it pulsated up into my throat. My heart was beating faster, throbbing through my mouth, through my ears, in powerful temple thumping blows.

The nurse quickly ran off to find Endone, fast acting morphine-like pain relief, similar to the Oxycontin I'd been taking. I couldn't help the moans that were escaping me. I couldn't shut up. The pain was stronger than me. 'Oh, please stop! *Please*! I don't want anymore *pain*!' I thought. It took so much inner strength to lower the volume of my screams that I had to hold my breath.

The nurse raced back to me, handing me the tablets and water. Urgently taking them with trembling hands, I couldn't wait for the relief! I looked over at the clock on the wall, desperately waiting for the alleviation. It was as if my body was sending a message, screaming at me, warning me of the danger spreading inside my chest.

My face began turning a mean shade of yellow as the rush of nausea started hitting me, with my mouth drying up, making it hard to swallow. Mel came in then, saw my face, and rushed around looking for a bucket. Oh, please, I don't want to vomit, not through this pain, I thought!

I begged for anti-nausea pills, and was given an injection instead. I knew the nausea was the awful side effects of these fast acting morphine tablets. The pain was throwing me into blasts of screams by this stage.

About five minutes later, I felt the dullness start to seep through the pain. I tried to take deep breaths, but that caused more severe stabs of sharp pain through my back and into my sides. I forced myself to relax and slowly breathe through it.

When the pain subsided, along came the peaceful high. Ohhh . . . it was wonderful. I was deliriously relieved.

In fact, I had not a care in the world. I hadn't felt this relaxed and happy in what seemed like aeons.

Relief from everything, including my own head. My thoughts had been switched off and that constant pressure of paranoia lifted. It helped me get through the rest of the afternoon.

While being sedated, I somehow managed to have so much energy and adrenaline running through my body. Feeling like my old self again, I was suddenly in a great mood! I realised then how much I missed being me.

Mel began telling me her own story, waiting for me in the cafeteria and falling asleep at the table in front of everyone, her head falling forward and nearly bashing the table. I was beside myself. She was the perfect person to be with on that day. With my new mood, I wanted to talk to Mel about everything; we had one month's worth of gossip to catch up on, but we weren't allowed. The nurse would come by, telling Mel to keep it down and let me rest, when I was the one doing all the talking. I was in stitches.

The afternoon went by fairly quickly, and I was finally allowed to go home. I couldn't wait to hold my kids!

But, from the medicated high, came the rapid, gut-wrenching, menacing fall.

The drive home was worse than the drive to the hospital—like Formula 1 on speed. Whether it was the medication making me feel this way, or Mel's driving, I had to physically hold on to my stomach to keep it down, as the wave of nausea repeatedly crashed over me. As the sedation became heavier I couldn't open my mouth to talk.

The switch in my head turned itself on again, like an AM radio shoved into my head that wouldn't turn off, raising the volume with an onslaught of questions driving me crazy. How long will the results take? What if the doctor was right, and the results come back inconclusive? What if the tumour continues to grow while I wait for the results? Is it becoming more aggressive? Could it be lymphoma, as the doctor had said? Will I need to go through chemotherapy? What if the chemo doesn't work? Can it spread onto my heart lining while we wait for results? Is it spreading anywhere else? Why all the pain? Why is it so intense? How long will I need to wait to get rid of it? Why am I going through this?

Oh, shut uuuuuup. My brain was combusting. While Mel was busy driving, I had too much time to think. The last thought that I had echoed through my head and tied knots through my insides: Am I going to make it through this? Just as my eyes were brimming with tears, I quickly wiped them away. Of course I am.

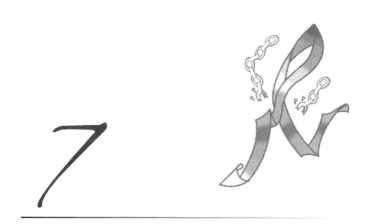

7

HOLD ON TO YOUR SUPPORT SYSTEM

Once I was home, I went straight to the couch to heal, recover, and think. My family didn't bombard me with questions. They left me alone. When I was ready, I began telling them about the day and what the doctor had said about the results. It frustrated them to no end that the doctor didn't agree with having the needle biopsy.

How long would it be before I could start fighting this thing?

I found myself in the waiting game again. This was the worst part about the whole process. It's like pressing pause on your life with the tumour still growing. I'd read about patients being admitted into hospital for surgery and biopsies almost immediately on knowing about their tumours. They were able to start their treatment with much shorter waiting times. So why the hell wasn't this the case for me?

Not knowing what was happening to me coupled with the symptoms worsening was my personal nightmare. My health started deteriorating fast in the coming days of waiting. Not only was I living with the chills, fevers, head pressure and body pain, the frustrating cough, struggling for deep breaths, exhaustion, and still sounding like a pubescent constipated chipmunk, but new symptoms started to appear.

Heart palpitations were the most terrifying. It felt like my heart was struggling to beat, particularly when I would lie down on my back. That's when I would feel the pressure the most. To feel my heart suddenly increase its palpitations, skip a beat, then jump back into beating fast and hard again was frightening. I became scared for my life, just hoping to wake up the next day.

Apart from the freezing chills, the night sweats had become severe. I would wake up drenched, like I had walked into the shower with all my clothes on. Paul had to sleep as far away from me as possible, as I would drench him as well. Perspiration would soak through my clothes, through the sheets, and onto the mattress, and we would have to get up every night before dawn to change. I've never seen anything like it and I couldn't believe all this water was coming out of my body.

My body wasn't coping with whatever it was that was taking over.

I could no longer lift my arms up above my head, especially my left arm. When I'd try to lift it, the tightness under my arm would involuntarily pull my arm down, with the tumour pushing against the side of my throat, strangling me. It was also becoming increasingly difficult to swallow.

Even with the Oxycontin and paracetamol, the ongoing pressure and jabs in the centre of my chest intensified. This thing was becoming a part of me.

Yawning, and sneezing, became a problem. I learnt to stop both in their tracks, absolutely dreading them. There was no more room in my chest for a deep breath, let alone a yawn or a simple achoo. Both were incredibly inconvenient. I would brace myself, and hold on to my chest, squeezing at my skin with my fingers. Anything to try to lessen the shooting jabs.

With all of the new symptoms quickly emerging, I felt the urgency a lot more, desperate for the results to come back quickly, hopefully conclusive. Hopefully with an answer. It was all I could think about.

With all of these symptoms, all I could imagine was the tumour growing and taking over.

September 2009

Finally the two weeks passed, and my mum and I were in the hospital waiting room again. We felt absolute relief when a different doctor called my name.

On the way to his office, my mother and I started our desperate plea for help. We began explaining everything I had been going through, right in the middle of the hallway. We didn't care about anyone around us or what we looked like. My mum grabbed his arm and begged him crying, 'Please help us! *Please* help her!'

He took us into an office, grabbing a box of tissues on his way since we had both fallen to pieces. I apologised for our sudden outburst, but he understood our desperation.

I calmed down and told him about the new symptoms that had appeared over the past weeks since the biopsy: that I couldn't lift my left arm up anymore; that I was no longer able to take in a deep breath, or even yawn or sneeze. However, when I mentioned the heart palpitations, he looked alarmed, and quickly disappeared out of the room.

Was that a good thing, or a bad thing? I thought. Who cares! He listened. I couldn't help but think that this was how I should have been treated from the beginning—with urgency. My mum and I were left in the room, quietly drying our tears, waiting.

We waited about fifteen minutes, and with every passing minute, our anxiety grew. What was happening? Had he forgotten about us?

No. The door opened, and a well-dressed man in a suit walked in. Straight away, he walked over to me and introduced himself with such a gentle manner and soft tone that threw me so off guard I nearly fell off my chair.

'Hi, Karina. My name is Professor Choong. I am a cardiothoracic surgeon. I understand that you're in a great deal of pain and have been waiting a while now for answers. I have looked at your file, and I would like to help you in finding what you need.'

Tears sprang to my eyes again as my emotions took the better of me.

'We need to do another biopsy, because the needle biopsy you had came back inconclusive.'

And I wasn't expecting anything more. Hoping, but not expecting.

'I'm quite surprised they put you through that in the first place. The size of your tumour is alarming, Karina. There are many different types of cancers and diseases that can cause tumours in the chest. In my experience, and because of its location, it looks to me like lymphoma, but we need to confirm that before you can start any treatment. Chemotherapy is the usual treatment regime for this type of blood cancer, but that's something you can talk about later with the appropriate specialists or oncologist.

'I'm going to be honest with you: this is a critical situation. What concerns me is the heart palpitations you're experiencing. I believe it's from the weight of the tumour causing stress on your heart, so we need to act quickly. I want to book you in for surgery one week from now. It's what we call major surgery. We will have to open your chest and cut through the muscles and tissues to get through to the tumour, from just above your breast.

'If we can't reach it from that direction, we will have to go in under your left arm and cut through that way to reach the tumour. I will try to reach it without cutting a rib, but if it becomes too difficult, we will have to cut through a bone. The cut will be about six to eight centimetres deep. But, there is also a risk. Looking at your scans, the tumour is wrapped around the major blood vessels surrounding your heart, with some vessels going through the centre of it. It's also wrapped around your oesophagus, while displacing it to the side.' Is that why I feel like something is strangling me?

He briefly showed me the scan images on the screen in front of him. Every time I saw it, it scared the hell out of me. I understood the difficulty in getting to the tumour, and I suddenly longed for a bucket.

He went on, 'The risk is that we could ultimately cut into one of these vessels, because while we are opening the chest we can't see what lies is in front of the scalpel. The tumour has moved your blood vessels from where they normally lie. If we do cut a vessel, it can create severe blood loss, and can ultimately cause death.

'My team and I will do our best to prevent this, of course, and we will be prepared for anything, but I need to inform you of all the risks before you agree to the surgery. There are risks in every surgery, but this procedure will be difficult. How do you feel about this?'

Well, where do I start? Dizzy, relieved, scared, confused, happy, anxious and determined.

'Let's do it,' I said. 'Either way, if I don't have the surgery, the tumour will kill me. So, I'm trusting you with my life.' And I meant it. I had only known him for less than twenty minutes, but I knew I was in safe hands.

My poor mum had been weeping quietly next to me the whole time, wiping her tears with her drenched tissue. I put my arms around her and told her we were on our way to an answer, squeezing her hand, wishing

I could take the hurt away from her. Finally. Professor Choong explained to me that I'd have to stay in hospital for two or three days after the surgery to recover and heal. Anticipation ruled over every other emotion. I just wanted my old life back.

'Karina, I don't often talk to my patients about this, but do you believe in god?'

My mouth dropped open in awe as I nodded. As much as I'd questioned Him through my life's ups and downs, I believed in God. Wait a minute, a surgeon talking about god?

He continued, 'You should say a prayer when you get home. Talk to Him. Ask Him to help us do what we need to do to save your life. Have faith in Him. He will give you the answers.'

I was speechless. I hadn't cried through the whole 'You could die through surgery' explanation, but I started crying then.

Even though I'm not an overly religious person, I do believe in God, and in that moment, I needed to hear that someone out there was watching over me.

Professor Choong booked me in for surgery in one week's time and I couldn't thank him enough as we signed the pre surgery forms. He extended his hand to shake mine, but what I really wanted to do was hug him. This humble man was going to help save my life. I owed him so much. I wished I had seen him in the first place.

He gave me his card before we left with his mobile number on it, and told me to call him if we had any concerns, or if my heart palpitations became alarmingly worse.

What an amazing man.

Mum and I broke down in the car. We were both so relieved that we could see the light at the end of the tunnel! My tears fell in streams down my face—tears of immense joy and relief. Even though I had only met Mr Choong briefly, I appreciated him for the incredible person he was and for helping me so quickly, for listening and taking me seriously.

Interrupting my small moment of euphoria, it hit me like a sucker punch in the guts that one of my kids could potentially develop this same disease if it was lymphoma. My research of the past few weeks indicated that lymphoma may possibly be genetic, but it's not entirely certain. My dad's sister had passed away from a type of blood cancer, but being forty years ago, and in a third world country, the doctors didn't know exactly what it was. I worried, and I still worry. I don't think I could handle seeing my kids go through this.

At that moment I looked over at my mum. I asked her how she had been coping from the beginning, even though I could see for myself how it was affecting her. Mum confessed to me that over the past few weeks, she broke down every morning on her way to work. She would scream while she drove, and beat the steering wheel, screaming, '*Why?*'

I choked back my own tears as she cried, 'It's not fair, Karina, I'm supposed to go before you. I *can't* bury you. You're my *baby*. I beg God every minute to take me instead of you. To choose *me* instead! I've already lived my life. You need to live yours! You're so young. You need to be there for your kids, to experience them when they're older. They *need* you. *Paul* needs you. *Why* is this happening to you, Karina? *Why you!* It's not fair. It's not *fair!*'

I held her hands, hopelessly looking into her eyes as she cried hysterically.

Seeing her like that killed me.

'This is my fault, Karina. Maybe I did something when you were growing up to cause this. This has to be my fault. You don't deserve this. I would give my life to fix this for you, to take this away from you. If I could, I would rip it out of you and put it in me. I would do it *right* now, Karina. I would do anything! *I don't want this for you!*'

The agony she was in pained me. Still holding on to her, wiping the solitary tear sliding down my face, I reassured her, 'Mum, you didn't do anything wrong. It just happened. As much as it hurts and as much as it might seem impossible right now, I need you to believe in me. Believe me that I will get through this. Since when do I ever give up on anything? You know me—nothing stops me. I wish I could stop it all now get rid of this crap inside my chest too, whatever it is. You've always said I'm stubborn like a brick wall. Well, for once in my life being stubborn is finally going to work for me, because it's in my head that I'm going to beat it, so I will. It chose the wrong person, Mum. We are all going to kill this son of a bitch together, okay?'

I held onto my breath seeing the grief spilling out of her. My mother was the one who taught me to be strong from such a young age, just by leading me through her own example of strength. And now her strength was crumbling.

I hated this. I hated how much pain I was putting my family through. It wasn't right. In the week leading up to the surgery, I immersed myself with my kids. We watched movies and pigged out on junk food. We spent as much time together as we could.

Nothing else mattered to me. I hugged them and held onto them, telling them how much I loved them and to never forget that they were my entire world.

Only during the night when I'd lie awake in bed would I allow myself to think about what was coming. When I'd feel the tears start to sting my eyes, I'd quickly breathe through it and force myself to fall asleep. I didn't want to cry anymore. I wanted to stay positive.

Two days before surgery, Professor Choong had booked me in for a pre-surgery appointment. During this appointment, I was to meet with an anaesthetist, and he would discuss the surgery and biopsy procedures with me, to prepare me for what was coming. I was to have some blood tests and a blood pressure check, and my heart rate would be monitored.

I was to ask any questions I had, but I couldn't think of any.

I went on my own, singing at the top of my lungs in the car all the way there. To say I was happy would be the understatement of the year.

At the hospital, the waiting time was lengthy, but I cherished those moments I had alone. I loved the silence. I didn't have to pretend to be anything.

I had my blood and urine tested. The anaesthetist then reviewed my medical history to determine what type of anaesthesia could be used on me. He physically examined me, pressing into my upper abdomen and my neck, checking my lymph nodes, my spleen and my liver with his hands.

I saw the scan images of my tumour again. This time, I asked if I could take a closer look. Seeing it so close and so clear, I swear I stopped breathing. I saw my blood vessels snaked through and around this gigantic ball. My curiosity turned into revulsion. I had to tell myself not to cry, and swallowed back the lump that started forming in my throat. This was what I was here for, I thought. I had to know. I wanted to be prepared. So deal with it, Karina.

When we finished talking, I had to have one more test. They wanted to trace my heart with something called an ECG machine: a small machine which graphically records the electrical activity of the muscles of the heart, used to identify the rate and regularity of heartbeats. The nurse hooked me up attaching electrodes to my chest, and a graph was gradually printed out. I'm such a pro, I thought, as I watched the printout, laughing at myself. I had to turn the bad into some sort of humour, otherwise I'd go nuts.

Given the all clear for my surgery, I whistled all the way down the corridors and went home, singing to myself, 'I'm having sur-ge-ry, I'm having sur-ge-ry, and nothing's stop-ping me, and nothing's stop-ping me!'

The day before the surgery, Paul called me from work. I knew straight away that something was wrong. 'Karina, I think you should make a will.' I didn't say anything. 'What if something happens to you? You have to think of the kids, baby. Think about it, just in case.'

A will? I wasn't expecting that one. I snorted. 'What do you mean?' I asked. His sudden declaration hurt me more than anything, not because he asked me to make a will, but for giving up on me before I had even begun my fight; for not having the faith in me that I could do this, that I could come out of this more alive than before.

'Nothing is going to happen to me, Paul. Why does everyone keep talking about death? I'll be fine!'

But it wasn't really my will that was bothering him. 'Karina, I don't know what I would do if anything happened to you. How am I going to raise the kids on my own? I don't want to be a single father. I can't do it without you. I need you.' His voice broke and I had to stop myself from falling apart with him.

Well, shit. I started doubting myself again. Just when I had found my inner strength, death was put in my head, but coming from Paul, it didn't anger me. On the contrary, I wanted to pull him out of his despair and support him, as he'd been supporting me.

'Paul, nothing is going to happen to me, but if it does, they have you. You're all they need.'

He remained quiet.

'Paul, if something does go wrong, you have to promise me that you'll tell them every day how much I love them. Tell them how much I wished I could have had more time with them. Especially Jaivan. He doesn't know me,' I said.

That did it—talking about my kids without a mother again tore at my heart.

Paul went on to say, 'Baby, if there really is a god, how could he do this to you? You're a good person! I don't understand, why *you*? How could He let this happen? You mean everything to me. How am I supposed to live without you? And the kids . . .' Paul went to pieces, and I went with him.

We stayed on the phone, as I silently cried from hearing him break. The uncertainty of where we were headed was the harsh reality of the chaos we were all being thrown into.

That conversation lingered in my head for the rest of that day. I hated how much this was affecting my entire family. I wished I could go through this quietly and undercover, without affecting anyone.

My dad looked apprehensive that afternoon, like he yearned to say something but didn't know how to approach me. He hadn't said much since it had all begun, sitting in his chair all day, every day, pensively staring out the window, and keeping to himself.

I was relieved when he finally built up the courage to get whatever was bothering him off his chest.

'Karina, your mother is suffering a lot with everything that's happening to you,' he said.

'I know,' I said as the guilt tugged at my heart and my gut.

'No, don't feel bad. I'm not telling you this to upset you. I just thought that you should know how worried she is, we both are. She loves you so much, Karina. We both do. We're your parents and it's hurting us to see you like this. It's normal.'

A tear slid down his face. Seeing him like that, my own tears started. He couldn't speak for a while, choked on his own anguish, and I didn't push him. He swallowed hard several times trying to compose himself and clear his throat. His tough facade finally crumbled.

'I am scared for you, Karina. I'm here with you every day—I see how sick you've become. I hope this surgery gives you the answer.' He nervously shook his head. 'I can't believe this is happening to you. How can you have cancer?' he asked. 'You're so young, and you're getting worse. Do you think it's growing, Karina'?

I couldn't answer that. He was going through enough. 'Dad, I'll be fine. You'll see. I'll be back to normal in no time. And, you know what? I want to write a book. I want to help other people going through this too.' I smiled and hugged him, wiping my tears away behind his back.

My dad doesn't show emotion much at all. The hardness of his life has taught him to present a tough shell to the world. But the tough exterior disguises the compassionate, caring and empathetic man he his on the inside. He was raised on the streets in Uruguay, South America, with his brothers. He was moulded to be fighter. Only the people close to him see who he really is.

I was relieved that the men in my life had finally started opening up to me. The last thing I needed was for any of my family to hide behind lies and masks. I wanted them to tell me everything they were going through, every emotion they were feeling. As hard as it was to face them like that, the honesty brought us closer together.

The night before surgery, I fell into a deep, peaceful sleep. My alarm woke us up, but I didn't want to get out of bed. Maybe I can have the surgery tomorrow, I thought.

My body felt heavy, my feet chained to the mattress. Even though I wasn't looking forward to the day that lay ahead because I had no idea what to expect, I leaped out of bed and talked myself into an adrenaline rush.

I wasn't allowed to eat breakfast before surgery, which didn't bother me because I wasn't hungry, only nervous and eager to get going. My head was empty of thoughts for once.

My mum was looking after my kids that morning so Paul could come with me to the surgery. I hugged my kids tight, holding them while saying a silent prayer in my head that this would not be the last time I would get to hold them.

I kissed them, squeezing them over and over into tight embraces and reassuring them I'd see them soon, before walking out the door.

The hardest part was seeing them crying at the door, watching us walk down the driveway to the car. My mum, holding Jaivan at the door, looked away so I wouldn't have to see the quiet tears rolling down her cheeks.

'Please come back, Mama,' said Monique, and both girls ran down the driveway, holding onto me one more time.

'Of course I'm coming back, guys,' I said. 'Don't worry, it's all going to be fine, and you guys can come by tomorrow and visit me at the hospital, okay?' They nodded.

'I love you, Mama,' Aaliyah cried out as I climbed into the car. Hearing those words was like balm for my soul, strengthening my unyielding determination.

Watching them go through their heartache was gut wrenching. I had to make it through this surgery, and I would, for them.

On the way to the hospital, I kept looking at the date on my phone. It was 28 September. Why was that date so familiar to me? As if answering the question in my head, Paul looked at me and said, 'Baby, happy anniversary. I love you.'

8

YOU CAN DO ANYTHING

Waiting at the hospital took forever and I was starving, silently cursing the bastard of a tumour for the upheaval it was creating.

It was unusual to be there so early while it was so quiet. Finally we were taken into the day ward, where other patients waiting for surgery like myself would wait. It reminded me of the orphanages you see in the old movies. Beds set up in rows, one after another, sad faces staring at us.

Adrenaline pumped through my insides with the unease of being there but I took it as a good omen to be having surgery on our wedding anniversary.

After the nurses prepared me with the hospital nametag and paperwork, Paul looked at me sadly. He crawled into the bed with me and held onto me, telling me over and over how much he loved me, kissing my face and holding my hands.

I held onto him with everything I had. We must look like lovesick teenagers, I thought, smiling.

'Baby, it's our wedding anniversary, and we really should be celebrating before you go into surgery, you know, because this could be the last time we're together,' he said.

'Yeah, we are celebrating,' I said blissfully, without a care in the world. 'This won't be the last time, Paul. I'm going to be fine.' I affectionately looked straight into his eyes, fighting back the build up of tears. It was so comforting lying in his arms, that I calmed down from the nerves of the morning.

Well, he chose that moment to snap me back into his own reality. 'Do you think anyone would notice if we made love right now, in this bed? We'd be under the covers.'

What? I burst out laughing! Typical! Seeing how serious he was about his offer made me laugh even more! For that short moment, we were just 'us'. No one and nothing else mattered.

The nurse came in then, and called my name.

My anxiety and nerves roared back up again. Here we go, I thought. I said goodbye to Paul, who wouldn't let go of me. He stared after me, not taking his eyes off me for a second while I was being wheeled away. I saw his pain and uncertainty, even through his smile. I didn't think going into surgery would affect him that way. He's always so calm and easy-going.

Oh, please, let me see him again.

They wheeled me into another ward, a type of holding area, where patients wait for their surgeries. We were alone, but surrounded by each other, if that makes sense.

This is it. This is really it. I will finally find out what has been making me so sick for so long.

I couldn't help but get excited while I waited, even though I was scared as hell.

As soon as I got comfortable, they called my name again. My emotions were bouncing around like a Ping-Pong ball.

They wheeled me into another room, and I had absolutely no idea where I was. I was completely alone in there. As usual, I panicked. What if I'm in the wrong room? What if they forget I'm here? Am I supposed to be here? Should I tell someone?

Telling myself to calm down, I closed my eyes and waited, dancing (well, moving) to the songs that were in my head.

I could hear the surgery going on in the room next to mine. They were trying to wake a patient, and I could hear him moaning in pain. That's going to be me soon. My anxiety shot through the roof. Shit.

No, Karina, just relax, damn it.

The anaesthetist came in and explained the process of knocking me out. 'As long as I wake up, do whatever you want to me,' I said, trying to crack a joke.

I asked him to double dose any anti-nausea meds because I'd heard how a general anaesthetic could cause vomiting on waking up. I hate vomiting.

Professor Choong came in then, said hello, and walked straight over to a bench filled with papers and other hospital equipment. I wondered what he was doing. His head was bowed down, like he was writing, but he didn't have a pen in his hand. He stayed that way for a couple of minutes, then lifted his head up and made the sign of the cross across his chest. He was praying? *Really*? Wait a second, he's praying for me?

Tears swelled in my eyes. I couldn't believe what I was seeing.

He came over to me, and explained to me again that the chance of dying on the table was high. He reminded me that he would be cutting through my flesh with no visibility as to what was lying in front of the scalpel—that the blood vessels surrounding the tumour had been moved around due to its size and growth.

He was deadly serious and amazingly honest.

Holding my hand, he told me to pray, not only for the surgery to go well, but to pray for him and his team: to pray that God would use their hands to serve as useful tools for me, to provide me with the answers I needed to save my life. To pray that the tumour would be easily accessible through the tangle of vessels, and that the ultrasound machine would give them enough of a clear window to what was inside.

Pray that they would be able to cut a good-sized piece of the tumour for a sample, and that if something should go wrong, he and his team would have sufficient help from Him to get me out of it. Pray that I wake up when it was over for my children . . . for my family.

I lost it. I smiled at him through the fog of tears and the massive lump in my throat, thanking him repeatedly, not used to having a complete stranger care about me the way he did.

Watching him walk back into the operating room, I had to talk myself into finding some sort of strength or courage. My hands were ice cold from fear and my mouth as dry as dust. I didn't want to go in there giving up before it had even started. I didn't want to be scared anymore. I wanted to be strong.

I visualised myself waking up after surgery, seeing Paul and holding my babies in my arms. I may not have known what to expect, but in that moment, I knew what I wanted. I wanted to live.

They wheeled me into the surgery theatre while the assistants were setting up. It was like a scene out of a movie. Switching off all surrounding sounds, I made myself stare at the ceiling, counting the tiles, as I listened to the humming of the air-conditioner. Believe it or not, it was soothing.

A nurse put some patches on my chest for the ECG machine to keep a trace on my heart. They clipped another machine onto my finger to measure my oxygen levels, and took my blood pressure. With all the nerve-wracking tension running rampant through my body, I may as well have been preparing to jump out of a plane . . . without a parachute.

The expected surgery time was one to two hours.

The anaesthetist came over to me then, and started talking and laughing with me about god only knows what, because I certainly can't remember. I felt relaxed and intoxicated all of a sudden, not worried about anything. He was fumbling around with the cannula that was inserted in a vein in my hand, connecting me to the IV. He told me to count to ten, and that was the last thing I remember.

★　　★　　★

Upstairs at home in my bed, in the best most peaceful, deepest sleep that I'd had in a very long time, my dad was calling me from downstairs.

'Karina. Karina, wake up, wake up.'

Completely annoyed, I was trying to yell back 'No! Le'me slee!' Lea'me 'lone!'

But my jaw was clamped shut, and I noticed something different about my voice. Was I mumbling? Not yelling? But I wanted to yell! I tried to open my eyes in a panic, but they were glued shut. I couldn't see. I couldn't breathe! What's going on? I tried to take in a deep breath, and I couldn't. 'I can't breathe . . . I can't breathe!' I mumbled as I gasped for air.

'Karina, can you hear me'? You're in the hospital. You just had surgery. Try to relax,' I heard.

'But I can't breathe! I can't breathe!' I mumbled back, trying to scream, but I couldn't. Sharp pains stabbed me everywhere!

It was like my lungs had no room. I couldn't even take in a shallow breath. I lifted my hand to my face, but my arm was tied down. What the hell is going on! Why can't I breathe! I was trying to open my eyes, trying to see and make sense of everything. Where was my dad? Wasn't he calling me?

Slowly, I began to remember where I was. The surgery was over? And I'm okay? I tried to tell whomever it was standing next to me through the agonizing gasps of air, that something sharp inside my chest was piercing me and I wanted to rip it out! She explained to me that I had lost a lot of blood during surgery, and they had had to put a drainage tube inside, beside my lungs, to drain any excess blood and fluid.

I could see her clearly now and burst into desperation, pleading with her to rip it out while still trying get some oxygen through the painful stabbing. I sensed some commotion around me as she started rushing around me, checking my pulse. She told me to breathe with her, slowing my pace, but the pain was unbearable.

A doctor came to me and I heard the nurse talking to him. Then I felt someone quickly pushing down on my chest, and felt more pressure increasing inside me. I opened my eyes to see a blurry figure pulling and tugging at the tube to loosen it inside. There's a tube inside of me? A wave of nausea hit me and my insides churned at seeing him pulling at it.

In a split second I could breathe. What a relief. I still had the tube in there, but it wasn't as painful as before.

Completely dazed and disoriented, I knew I was in the hospital, but where? What part? Straight away I looked around for Paul and asked the nurse where he was. 'I'll find out for you,' she said. 'Are you okay now, Karina'?

I tried to nod, but I was so stiff that I couldn't move. My eyes were the only part of me I could move. The nurse told me to rest and gave me something in my hand with a button. She told me to press it whenever I felt pain, explaining that it was my own morphine control. When I pushed the button, the pain relief would be delivered into my vein through the IV.

Well, that got my attention! A handheld morphine remote control! (The technical term is patient controlled analgesia.)

Wait a minute, I feel fine, I thought. I did it! *He* did it! I went through my first major surgery! *I made it!*

I tried to sit up in my own personal euphoria, but the stabbing pain brought me crashing back down again. Ow! I lifted my left arm slightly and saw all the tubes connected around it. No wonder I felt tied down.

They kept me in this recovery room under observation for a couple of hours before I was allowed to go anywhere.

Armed with my remote, I was on top of the world! Nothing could get me. I loved being pain free and in control of it for once. I loved the idea of not having to wait for someone to bring me pain medication.

I asked the nurse if she could somehow let Paul know I was fine. I knew he'd be worried, and when I looked up at the clock on the wall, I couldn't comprehend what I was seeing. Had it really been four hours?

I looked around to try to see any familiar faces, anyone from the other wards I had been in during the wait in the morning, but my vision was hazy beyond ten metres. I forced my body to relax and wait, to forget about everything. I was just happy to be awake with my morphine. I couldn't wipe the smile off my face, in a blissful ecstasy. I loved being alive!

After a while they finally rolled me out to the ward I was supposed to stay in for the next two or three days.

Good times being escorted by so many people. Yeah, definitely still high on morphine.

I heard Paul call out to me, and suddenly he was next to me, walking alongside the bed. His eyes were red and watery. Groggily, I smiled up at him.

Oh, please, don't cry, baby, I said in my head.

In my room, I phoned my family and hearing their voices put me at ease. Feeling peaceful with a huge weight being lifted off my shoulders, and knowing results weren't far off, I went into a deep sleep with Paul by my side.

Sharp stabbing chest pains woke me up hours later. Searching desperately for the morphine control at my side, I pressed the button with all my strength, which wasn't much, and in a matter of minutes, I couldn't feel anything again. This was awesome. I wished I could take it home with me.

With Paul still sitting beside me, I drifted off again, feeling completely safe and content.

Paul woke me to say goodbye when visiting hours were over. Suddenly alone, I had time to think and process what I had just been through, to focus on me—something I wasn't exactly used to.

It was hard to sleep during the night in that ward. I was surrounded by older patients, with one suffering from dementia. I felt so sorry for her as she would go into terrified screaming fits from fear of strangers, which is what the nurses were to her.

After finally falling into a deep sleep, I woke up abruptly in the middle of the night with a tremendous need to go to the toilet. Oh, how was I supposed to do that?

Pressing the morphine remote before calling anyone (just in case), I waited until I was completely dulled to any pain. I called a nurse and introduced myself (well, she was going to help me pee), and she suggested a bedpan. What a weird feeling, putting something under your butt to pee in, on the bed. At least I didn't have to get up. My dignity was slowly diminishing.

When she left I gradually began taking in my surroundings. I noticed I had tubes up my nose. How did I not notice that before? I looked around my bed and saw the bag of blood connected to the tube running into my lungs. It was huge and nearly half full.

I began replaying the surgery in my mind, still in some sort of disbelief, and slightly disappointed that I hadn't seen any white lights, or visions of a peaceful and mystical heaven. Turning on the TV to distract myself, I fell asleep to the humming of voices.

Early the next morning, a student doctor came in to talk to me about the surgery. She explained that they'd been pleased with the size of the sample they were able to get. They had to go in and cut numerous little pieces to create the size they needed, and after four hours they were able to do it. Realising she was a student, I wondered if she would be as closed off as the more senior doctors. I'd noticed that when I'd ask a doctor about my condition, they were really good at evading an answer, keeping it to the bare minimum of 'wait and see'.

Stupidly wanting more details, I asked her what it looked like in there, a question I should never have asked. She began explaining how hard it was for them to see where they were going, that blood vessels were all around it. That it was a mess.

Okay, I could handle that. Then I asked her what the tumour looked like. 'Like a big lump of black mess, like black jelly,' was the enthusiastic answer.

A what? I swallowed hard.

All I could do was picture the 'black mess'. Her description hit it home for me, slamming the image into my head, and forcing me into the raw truth. I bit down hard on my lip, trying to stop myself from crying. The image plunged into my mind again and again. It's one thing to say, 'I have cancer,' but a whole different thing to know it's for real.

Damn it, I couldn't stop the tears.

She noticed I was crying and suddenly looked panicked and almost horrified with guilt. I tried to hide my face behind my hands, and apologised for falling apart. It wasn't her fault. She left quickly and I felt terrible. I should never have asked those questions. I thought I was ready to hear the answers, but, honestly, nothing could have prepared me for that.

I looked at the tubes that were running from inside my chest to the bag of blood and fluid hanging on the side of my bed, and allowed myself to cry for as long as I could. This is real. Every little thing I had to go through was one step closer, and the tubes provided more evidence.

I pulled the smaller tubes out of my nose, but it was harder to breathe without them. I put them back in and slowly took in a deep breath, feeling the pain deep inside, next to my lung where the tube was sitting. Yes. It's not a dream anymore.

With my emotions hovering on the surface, I was a mess. Although I was well aware I'd have these moments, it infuriated me when I did, because I felt weak. I felt stupid for letting it all get to me like this, for being uncontrollably emotional instead of being 'positive' like everybody, including myself, kept telling me to be, or expecting me to be. I cried for the longest time, glad I could deal with this on my own. I couldn't handle anyone else right then—I couldn't even handle myself.

The only distraction I had was the TV. The commercials played some soft, sentimental music. It was a funeral ad. How appropriate. Perfect for the mood I was submersed in.

Paul came by that afternoon with our kids and my parents. Even though I was happy to see everyone, I was lost in my own inner thoughts. I avoided telling them the description of what the tumour looked like, although it was burning into every part of my brain.

I was in pain, uncomfortable and un-showered and just wanted to lose myself in the TV.

Despite craving solitude, I was grateful to my family. I could only imagine what it must have been like for them to see me that way. The tubes and the bag of blood and fluid scared the crap out of me, and it must have been the same for them. As the day was ending, the light at the end of the tunnel looked bleak.

Alone again, I sank into a depression. I looked like a mess, I smelt, I felt dirty, my mouth was a dry paste and I didn't care. I just wished for my life back to the way it was.

The next day, I pulled myself out of the oblivion I was in, and took a long, hot shower, brushing my teeth three times and using half a bottle of mouthwash. Professor Choong came by to check on me. He was pleased with the surgery, and reassured me that we should have the results in two weeks. He checked over my tubes, and told me they would be removing the draining tube that afternoon. Well, that made my day.

That afternoon, after pumping me with morphine from my remote control, the nurse prepared me for the removal of the drainage tube, and when it was finally out, I could semi-breathe again.

October 2009

When the day came to leave hospital, another nurse showed Paul and I how to keep the wound clean, and wished me luck. I noticed the nurses smiling sadly at me, and I found myself reassuring them that I was going to be fine. I couldn't help but laugh to myself.

My mini vacation was over. Armed with more medications—Oxycontin, Tramadol (more pain relief), paracetamol; Somac (for heartburn created from all the pain relief); and two types of laxatives (to treat the constipation from the pain relief)—we left.

The time was coming to kick cancer's arse, and I couldn't have been happier.

9

TAKING BACK CONTROL

What an amazing feeling it was to go home and see my family. Even though I was grateful for the break and the alone time, I appreciated how important it was to have them surrounding me again.

My extraordinary support team began expanding as the journey went on.

The day after arriving home, I went in to see Dr Raj. He checked my surgery wound, cleaned it and changed the dressing, and offered to do this for me every second day so I wouldn't need to stress about the wound. The nurses also began going out of their way for me, a support I was extremely grateful for.

It meant the absolute world to me.

Since showering was becoming increasingly difficult to do without wetting the bandage, I had to resort to bathing instead. My girlfriend Tracy, who also happens to be my hairdresser, offered to wash my hair as many times as I needed.

One morning, while Tracy washed my hair, she asked me how I was coping. It was strange to open up to her, as I was so used to masking my emotions around everyone. But, fighting back tears, I had a confession. 'Trace, sometimes I can't help question why this is happening to me?'

Trace looked at me and replied, 'You know what? I believe God gives the hardest battles to his toughest soldiers, to the people that are strong enough to handle it . . . strong enough to fight it. He's strengthening you for something else, Karina. It's like, He chose *you*.

'Believe you're strong enough, for yourself, and whatever happens at the end of it all, at least you know in your heart that you never gave up. You can do it, Karina. You're so going to come out of this. You're a strong woman. You should be proud of yourself. Not many people could keep going the way you have been.' I wept quietly, hoping she wouldn't see my tears run in with the water as she rinsed my hair, because I had never thought of it that way. And I carried her words with me through the rest of my journey.

Later in the week on one of my research tangents, I read somewhere that lymphoma is the 'good' cancer, and honestly, I found that completely stupid. There's no such thing as a 'good cancer' for the person having to fight it. Not when your whole life gets thrown upside down and everything you've lived for changes and halts in a heartbeat.

I came across blogs written by chemo patients and became obsessed reading about what a typical day was like for them, while at the same time scaring the crap out of myself. Some were handling treatment really well, but for others it sounded like a real battle in a war.

So, I chose to live life completely oblivious to cancer in those two weeks of waiting.

I went to dinner with friends a couple of times, but the pressure of the tumour would strangle me around my throat. I'd sit there trying to get into the conversation while subtly digging my fingers into my neck trying to push the tumour to the side. The tumour around my oesophagus was driving me mad.

And the coughing drove me nuts! I couldn't talk without coughing up my lungs. It was easier just to keep my mouth shut. People hearing me cough would stare in disgust, like I had some awful contagion, which would make me laugh, on the inside. I'd sit there, daydreaming that I march right up to them and politely inform them that I'm not contagious. I have cancer. Then smugly watch their reactions of shock and guilt. As much as I didn't want to be seen as a victim, I also didn't want to be shoved into a corner of diseased outcasts. If only they knew.

Despite that, with the added surge of fatigue, plus trying to raise what was left of my voice for it to be audible, I was determined to keep my life as normal as I could.

Looking around the restaurant, I remembered being there only a few months earlier and being absolutely normal. Pre symptoms. Those symptoms were the nonstop warning that it was growing. Honestly, deep down it scared me to death.

Not wanting to ruin the evening, I brushed it all off and coerced myself into having a good time, and eventually, I did.

Even though I continued to see Dr Raj to have the wound cleaned and dressings changed, an infection developed on the inside of the wound and I was given antibiotics. During the day, I regressed, weakening almost immediately, and felt extremely run down. I sweated profusely and turned pale with dark circles under my eyes.

The antibiotics worked over two days, and along with the Oxycontin and the anticipation of finding out the results, it was easier to start smiling again.

Two days before 'results' day, I went out to lunch with my parents, determined to enjoy every moment of life. During lunch, we talked and then, of course, we cried. I opened up about how I'd been feeling through the last couple of months and so did they.

Seeing how serious our conversation was getting, my son decided to stick straws up his nose. We burst into laughter watching this little person that sees the world so innocently, purposely lift our mood.

I laughed so hard, I felt like throwing up. Suddenly, I couldn't get the smallest gasp of air into my chest, rapidly asphyxiated by a wheezing and choking attack from the back of my throat. My mum rushed to my side, trying to give me water, but I wasn't choking on food. I was choking on the tumour.

I tried a deep breath again, with pain piercing through the side and middle of my chest and around my throat. The shock of it winded me. I got up, trying to look normal but it didn't work. In the midst of suffocating and coughing up my lungs and my food, I ran to the toilet with every eye in the restaurant following me.

It took so much to stop myself from throwing up. 'No! Screw you, you ugly piece of *shit*! You're *not* winning this!' I screamed in the bathroom. 'You're *not* going to ruin my day!'

Desperate to breathe, I tried to take as many shallow breaths as I could with the sharp pain wedged into the middle of my spine, digging deep into my left side. The morphine was failing and deep breaths were a thing of the past.

I tried to calm down. I couldn't wait to start chemo, if that's what it would take. Anger erupted inside me as I stared at my chest in the mirror. To think there was something sitting inside there and there was nothing I could do. If only I could physically get in there and rip it out myself!

I'd had enough. I'd been living with symptoms and feeling like crap for two months and it was *enough*. Feeling sullen and pissed off, we went home. I hated it. It was just a 'thing' to me, nothing more, and I was furious that this 'thing' was ruining my day, let alone ruining my life. I was sick of being blasé about it. I was sick of walking around like it wasn't bothering me anymore. I was done. And that anger fuelled the determination simmering just under my skin.

At the hospital on 'results' day, Mum and I couldn't contain ourselves. We just about skipped down the hospital corridors, eager for answers.

When I gave my name to reception, I expected to be one of the first called, since the results would be in. No point in waiting and prolonging it, right? Wrong. Another thing I learnt besides patience: go with the flow. Don't expect.

Watching other patients being called in to their appointments was torture. Three hours of torture. I could feel the next dose of Oxycontin was close and I hadn't brought any tablets with me thinking we wouldn't be waiting long. The pain faintly crept through my spine, and I quietly panicked. They should have me on record as a morphine junkie, I thought.

We were finally called, but the doctor looked far from happy. There were no results. Waiting all that time for nothing was a huge let down. To go from an epic high to a crashing low was cruel. I smiled, thanked him, and we walked to the car, shoulders slumped, heads down in complete silence. I had to wait another week.

Any more than that and I'd end up needing some serious therapy.

Besides the disappointment of having no results, I was left facing another battle. Constipation from all of the pain medications. The laxatives the hospital had given me provided absolutely no relief.

So, I decided to buy the next best thing—an enema. Never having used one before, and saying goodbye to any form of dignity I had left, I used it, and had to use it every couple of days afterwards.

Problem number twenty-something solved.

The following day I had a PET scan and a CT scan to go to. In the waiting room sitting next to me was a cancer patient wearing a wig. Seeing her with no eyelashes and no eyebrows, with the wig dancing on her hairless scalp, a part of me couldn't wait to join her—to be killing cancer. I had an urge to talk to her and bombard her with questions, but I didn't. I would be a part of her world soon enough.

After the CT scan, the dye must have reacted with the tumour, because the body aches and chest pains ripped through the Oxycontin. Desperately searching for my medication in my bag, I hoped the biopsy results would be ready at the next appointment.

Going in to the hospital for that appointment wasn't exactly excitement central. We didn't get our hopes up in case there were no results again.

Nonetheless, we weren't there for long when a different doctor called me in.

As soon as we sat down, he introduced himself as an oncologist. A what? He opened up my records and confirmed the test results had come back as Hodgkin disease, also known as Hodgkin lymphoma, and handed me the results of both scans from the week before. He would be overseeing my diagnosis, treatment schedule and fortnightly appointments.

He described lymphoma as being divided into two types, Hodgkin and non-Hodgkin, with many subtypes included in those. The one I had was the 'good' cancer, the one you hoped to get if you had a choice. Let me just say that any type of cancer sucks and if I had the choice, I wouldn't have got it in the first place. However, Hodgkin is the 'best' because it responds well to chemotherapy.

Chemotherapy. Shit.

He explained that lymphoma is a cancer that affects the lymphatic system. The cancer grows when developing lymphocytes (a type of white blood cell) form a malignant change and multiply uncontrollably.

This then increases the number of abnormal lymphocytes, called lymphoma cells, and a collection of cancer cells, or tumours, accumulate in the lymph nodes. Lymphoma cells gradually replace normal lymphocytes, which can weaken the immune system and the body's ability to fight infections.

He confirmed all the symptoms I had were part of the disease.

The combination of chemotherapy drugs used is made up of four different drugs called ABVD: Adriamycin (doxorubicin); Blenoxane (bleomycin); Velban (vinblastine); DTIC (dacarbazine).

The required dosage was one treatment every two weeks over the next five to six months. There would be twelve treatments in total broken into six cycles (two treatments per cycle).

As if a block of ice had hit me in the face, I stiffly nodded, dizzy from all the numbers and cycles as he continued explaining.

One of the drugs was known to possibly cause changes to lung tissue or lung damage. Another one was known to cause heart problems. Anything else, I thought? I had no idea that while chemotherapy is effectively fighting the cancer cells, it can potentially be harmful to the other organs in the body.

I was classified as Stage 4B, because it had spread onto the lung it was touching. Hearing Stage 4, I wanted to burst into tears. That sounded terrible, like a death sentence. Why couldn't I be a Stage 1, at least? The 'B' classification was due to the lymphoma symptoms I had developed. I couldn't believe how cunning this type of cancer was, masking itself behind flu-type symptoms, almost like on purpose, to trick us all until it completed its mission.

After chemo, one month of radiation treatments would be a possibility. If successful remission was reached after treatments, five years of further tests and scans would follow to ensure successful remission is maintained. However, he explained that a time frame of eleven years of full remission is considered to be 'safe' from disease.

Eleven years? Longer than most other cancers due to lymphoma being a type of blood cancer.

Dr Stephen Opat—head of Clinical Haematology, explains the following regarding remission:

The chance of relapse goes down over time. The greatest risk is in the first two years, with over 95% cured at 10 years post treatment.

After 10 years, the risk of recurrence is very low (5%). However, it is also important to be aware of the small risks of late side effects from treatment; including bone marrow damage from chemotherapy, and breast cancer in women who've received radiotherapy.

And this is the 'good' cancer?

So, basically, I'd be in my forties before I could *really* celebrate remission, and that's *if* treatment was successful?

What alarmed me the most was that the mass, being bulky (as it is referred when it's a larger size), led him to believe that the tumour had been growing for approximately thirteen to sixteen months. This meant that this tumour had started growing half way through my pregnancy with Jaivan.

My arid mouth turned to stone as I slowly felt the blood drain from my face. My mum asked him if Jaivan had any chance of having traces of cancer cells in his body. She grabbed my nervous hand with sheer terror in her eyes. He explained that it wasn't possible because cancer cells are too large to cross through the placenta to the baby.

Letting out a sigh of relief, I couldn't help the panic rising on the inside. It's enough that I had to go through it, but not my son. I wouldn't know what to do with myself. Pangs of guilt stabbed at my heart as I swallowed back the dry knot building in my throat.

Had it really been growing for the past thirteen to sixteen months? While he quickly ran through some of the chemo side effects, I couldn't help but ask myself, what had I done wrong? Did I cause this? Was there something I did during my pregnancy that created the tumour? Was this my fault?

'So, that's it then. I have to start the fight for my life,' I said, trying to supress the ache of threatening tears. I was being thrown into this against my will. All the amount of research, devastating images of scans, and waiting around for results over the past months could never have prepared me for the reality I was confronted by in that moment.

'Karina, don't look at it that way. The survival statistics are great with Hodgkin's. It responds really well with chemo. Most lymphoma patients look forward to their chemotherapy because the alleviation of their tumour symptoms far outweighs the chemo symptoms. You'll be feeling better in the first two or three treatments,' he said.

To be pain free, cough free, sweat free, and comfortable in my own skin again was my greatest desire and the belief in myself escalated.

Before starting chemo, I was to have a bone morrow biopsy to determine if any lymphoma cells were present in the soft tissue inside my bones. But we were running out of time. And secretly, I didn't want to know if any cells had raided my marrow. If they had, the chemo would destroy them anyway.

He booked me in for the end of the week, so I had three days left. Wait, three days? Oh shit!

We drove home thrilled that we finally had answers and a green light to start destroying cancer. It was an incredible feeling—a step forward to freedom.

Through the night, I couldn't sleep. The thought that cancer was on a rampage in my body while I was roughly five months pregnant continued to bother me, sickening me with worry and guilt.

How could I have let this happen? Not even Paul could understand why I was feeling so guilty, or why I was blaming myself. My son was fine.

The scan report confirmed what I'd heard and seen through the investigations: 'The large soft tissue density mass does surround three major blood vessels arising from the aortic arch.' Looking through the images, that bastard looked massive to me.

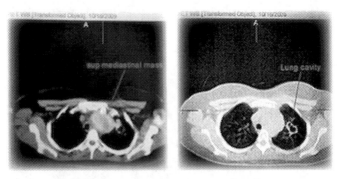

Lymphoma mass   Lung lesion

The lung on my left side was completely squashed and deformed.

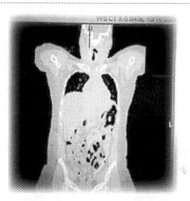

Full body PET scan

Wanting to find some way to help my body through cancer and treatment, (if there was any), I began another internet search about lymphoma linked with successful alternative treatments and natural therapies. I found that the most supportive and proven treatments were Chinese medicine and acupuncture.

I read about studies conducted by medical doctors and researchers who had investigated the results of Chinese medicine and acupuncture on cancer patients treated by chemotherapy and radiation. The results indicated that integrating the two with oncology treatment could strengthen and regulate the immunity of cancer patients, and significantly lessen the side effects of chemotherapy and radiation.

Nourishing the blood, clearing toxic heat, and protecting liver and kidney function were just some of what I read about. Having a professional and registered Chinese medicine practitioner prescribe a potent herbal formula specific to a patient's requirements, medical history and symptoms could be effective.

The next day, I found a registered practitioner, Dr Louis Cali, in my area. I drove to his clinic immediately without making an appointment, and even though he was extremely busy, he made the time to see me.

I began telling him of my diagnosis with lymphoma, and he instantly began explaining why the lymphatic system develops cancer cells and tumours, also explaining how cancer is formed in the body through inflammation-causing factors like poor diet and stress. He was aware of the type of chemo regime I was facing, while being sincere and empathetic to my needs. He put me at ease immediately, because he knew what he was talking about.

To explain how Chinese medicine works, Dr Cali generously contributed the following information for this book:

> In Chinese medicine, a well-functioning gut is how the body makes blood (in other words, proper nutrition, digestion and absorption). Chemo damages the stomach, which is why chemo patients often experience nausea, vomiting and ulcers, and it also destroys the immune system, which in turn depends on strong blood. Herbs that strengthen digestion and stimulate blood are the key to a strategy of staying strong throughout chemotherapy treatment.

Herbs have been consistently shown to keep patients strong, improve energy levels, keep immunity strong, help with sleep, alleviate side effects of drug therapy, and help promote faster recovery from surgery, chemotherapy and radiotherapy.

Acupuncture is a time-tested and well-documented treatment for many of the symptoms and discomforts of cancer and cancer treatment. Pain is a major problem with cancer sufferers. Acupuncture is used to manage pain from surgery, tumours, chemotherapy and radiotherapy. It can also help with immune system irregularities.

Acupuncture is also used successfully for nausea, vomiting, dryness in the mouth and throat, diminished appetite, sleeping disorders, fatigue, stress and digestive problems (such as diarrhea, constipation, gastritis and abdominal pain). These are common complaints seen with individuals undergoing cancer treatment.

Dr Cali had worked with cancer patients before and had seen the positive results of alleviated chemo symptoms with his patients, therefore believing that mainstream and alternative medicines can work *together* for the benefit of the patient.

He was realistic, never once promising me that the herbs would save my life. He didn't give me any illusions of magic potions or false hope of life-changing remedies. Only help. And I liked the notion of having some control over what was going into my body, to help it in any way I could.

His treatment strategies were not designed to replace conventional oncological treatment, but rather complement it.

According to Dr Cali, I had to take two formulas, one specialised for my type of chemotherapy, and the second to help support and clear my lymphatic system. Because they had to be ordered specially I had to wait a week or two, which was fine with me because I hadn't started treatment. Every fortnight, a week after chemo, I would see Dr Cali for acupuncture.

I left feeling comfortable and confident that I was doing the right thing for my body.

The following day I went to have a pulmonary function test, where I found out my lung capacity had been affected due to the size of the mass. After that I bounced in to the chemo ward for my orientation day.

They took me into a private room where I didn't see anyone getting their chemo, which was probably a good thing. Ignorance was bliss.

The nurse gave me heaps of information regarding my treatment and symptoms I'd experience throughout my treatment. The Leukaemia Foundation provided easy-to-understand patient booklets about lymphoma and its treatment. There were also other information sheets and books in the pack about living with lymphoma.

The side effects I read about were: decreased blood cell production with a possibility of causing anaemia, leukopenia (decreased white blood cell counts, which may increase the risk of other infections, the most common in chemo patients being pneumonia), and thrombocytopenia (decreased platelets), meaning less blood clotting cells in the blood stream.

If I developed chills, shivers, shakes, or high temperatures above 38°C, I was to run to the nearest hospital.

Also mentioned were allergic reactions: rash; itching; redness; pain; dizziness; feeling anxious; wheezing; shortness of breath; and nausea and vomiting that may develop during treatment. I was to alert the nurses if any of those were felt. Changes in urine colour turning red or orange would occur up to twenty-four hours after chemo.

Fatigue from the decreased blood cell counts, insomnia from the steroids given to lymphoma patients, weight gain from an increased appetite also due to the steroids, mood swings (dark days were said to include sadness, anger, anxiety and depression), pain/swelling at the injection site, constipation, diarrhoea, stomach ulcers, mouth sores or ulcers, hair loss, scalp burning/itching or pain, dizziness, shortness of breath, and heart palpitations.

The list went on: flu-like symptoms, muscle pain and headaches, increased risk of sunburn (both during and after treatment), nail and skin discoloration, tingling, numbness or pins and needles in hands and feet, irregular menstrual cycles, infertility, and lower or higher libido (a higher libido would be a bonus for Paul).

The things that go through my head.

In particular, women could also expect hot flushes, dry skin, vaginal dryness, and other menopausal symptoms such as irregular or no periods.

There was an increased risk of bruising or bleeding due to low platelets, which meant no shaving or waxing as excessive bleeding from cuts can occur when platelets are too low. That was fine with me. I had a medical excuse not to shave my legs and look like an Amazon for the next six months.

The nurse explained in detail about the medication they would give me to help alleviate some symptoms: two different types of anti-vomiting pills; anti-nausea pills; laxatives; Gastro Stop (to stop diarrhoea); and more pain relief. I couldn't wait to be cancer clear.

Besides the side effects, there were long-term effects to be aware of such as infertility, secondary cancers, heart disease, slight risk of a heart attack, and lung damage. Hmph.

I was encouraged to inform the doctors or nurses if herbs, vitamins, anti-oxidants, and so on, are taken during treatment. I mentioned my herbs to her, and she told me to bring them in to my first visits so they could write down each ingredient.

Besides the extremely long list of everything that could go wrong, chemo sounded like a breeze! Well, sort of. Six months wasn't that bad. Looking back now, it really isn't that long a time, considering. It's shorter than a pregnancy and *that* was long enough. If I could do that three times, this should be easy. I went home beaming.

Among all the forms I had been given, there was a wig pack with an order form. No, I couldn't see myself wearing a wig. With baldness associated with cancer, I would wear a shiny scalp with pride. Nothing was going to get me down.

The Leukaemia Foundation was a major point of contact. Because lymphoma is a blood cancer, the foundation dedicates its time to support cancer patients with leukaemia, lymphomas, and myelomas.

I read through the long list of assistance they provide to cancer patients, and was surprised with all of the services. Emotional support and counselling; education programs; providing accommodation to patients in rural areas and who may need it during treatment, with on board medical staff to assist patients' needs; transport and courtesy cars; financial support; house keeping; child minding . . . the list was endless.

The day before treatment, the Leukaemia Foundation phoned to ask if I required any help or assistance with absolutely anything. Being surrounded by family, I didn't want to take advantage of their services, so I declined. To my surprise, I was sincerely reassured on the phone that I wasn't alone through my journey and I could contact them at any time during the course of treatment if I needed any help. The fact that they had no idea who I was, yet cared enough to call me was incredible. It was comforting to know I belonged to a group of people, that I wasn't alone.

In preparation for chemo, I had a blood test to ensure my red cell and white cell levels were good and ready for treatment. Four tubes of blood later with a tiny non-painful jab would become the norm before every treatment for the following six months, which didn't bother me at all. Just something more I had to adjust to.

Anticipating chemo the next day with Paul coming with me, I was brimming over with excitement!

So, why did I wake up panicking the next day?

The first morning of chemo I was a nervous wreck. Reality was smacking me in the face along with the fear of the unknown. My whole body was chilled to the bone, from my fingers down to my toes. I felt like I was strapped to an anchor, and every step was as heavy as lead. 'I can't do this,' I thought. 'I can't go through with this. I can't go and have chemo. Maybe I can cancel it, or avoid it. But how? I had no choice.

I went through all the motions of a typical morning, which kept me busy enough to hide the desperation, even from myself. My insides churned as my eyes grew wider than normal with anticipation. Panic, anxiety and fear of the unknown all rolled into one huge ball. Caught in this sinister shark's mouth, chemotherapy was now inevitable and in a few short hours I was to go through it. Just as I had thought I was ready, I wasn't. I was petrified.

Yesterday, I had cancer. Today, I was a cancer patient, whatever that meant. This would be a day I would never forget.

10

FIND YOUR POWER

On the way to the hospital I dissolved into tears. The word chemotherapy repeatedly whispered through my head. It was something so strange to me. Something I'd never experienced before or thought I'd ever have to deal with, and here I was on my way to face it. I couldn't stop my tears. I felt helpless and furious with my body all over again. I couldn't wrap my head around the whole six months treatment thing.

I turned the radio off. It was too much noise that I didn't have patience for. Looking out the window I shook my head in disbelief. I couldn't believe the past two months had come to this

I suddenly felt trapped. Claustrophobia clouded my head and I couldn't breathe. The inside of the car was closing me in, suffocating me while I cried into my hands. My heart was racing, with every beat thrumming in my ears. I wanted to turn the car back.

I frantically considered opening the car door mid-highway, and running to hide away somewhere, to escape what was coming. I didn't want to go through with this. I wanted to go home! I wanted to wake up from this nightmare that had become my life!

Crying harder, I couldn't hold it in any more. I looked over at Paul, realising he'd been completely silent through my break down. He had tears pooling in his eyes but he was holding onto them. I don't know how he did it. How he could hold it together completely blew me away. I wanted to stop crying and be there for him so much, but I was weak and crying too hard. I had absolutely no control.

I couldn't speak. He held my hand and told me to let it out, to keep crying for as long as I had to. He didn't tell me to shut up, and he didn't tell me to stop. He didn't judge me or criticise me, or get annoyed. He gave me that moment to do what I needed to do.

As soon as I'd dry my tears, the uncontrollable bawling started again. The drive to the hospital was just under an hour in peak traffic but felt eternal. I wished I could be in an induced coma for the next 6 months, and wake up when it was over.

When we arrived I couldn't move. I was glued to my seat. I glanced out the window towards the entry doors, and I couldn't face going in. My stomach turned again because I *knew* that this was it. Paul came over to my side of the car and opened the door. 'Come on, baby, they're waiting.' Senselessly shaking my head, I took his hand as he helped me out of the car, but everything was happening in slow motion.

We walked into the hospital, as I dragged my feet around to the chemo ward entrance. When we reached the ward doors with the words 'Chemotherapy Unit,' I stopped. I couldn't go on any further, paralysed and slammed into an invisible wall. Time stopped. Everything just stopped. I couldn't walk through those doors. It's not that I didn't want to, I physically couldn't.

I stood there listlessly, staring at those words with the smell of the antiseptic invading my nose, sickening me to the core until I burst into tears again. 'I can't do it, Paul! Please, don't make me! Don't make me go in there! I didn't ask for this! Please! I can't do it. *I can't*!' I moaned into his chest as he held on to me.

'Cry, baby, let it out.'

After a while, Paul held my face, drying my eyes. 'Baby, it's either this or nothing. If you don't do this, it's going to take you. I'll lose you. You have to be strong. Think of us. Think of the kids.'

'I know,' I wailed, but it didn't make it any easier to think of the kids. I wished that for just one second, I could be completely immune to the crippling fear. Wearily holding on to my husband, I pulled myself together and, wrapped in his arms, we walked through the doors.

When we reached the waiting room, I looked around and took notice of everyone else. My new world. I saw the other patients differently. Strangely enough, I had a sense of belonging, knowing that everyone around me was going through the same hell I was. That was sort of comforting, in a way.

There were patients of all ages, different races and sexes, with partners, without partners. I understood right then that cancer does not discriminate. The disease can happen to absolutely anyone. I started to envy the patients that would have surgery to remove their tumours, instead of having chemo. Most of them had the advantage of recovering, and getting on with their lives as if nothing had happened, with the freedom of not having to deal with chemotherapy.

I didn't believe for one second that Lymphoma was 'the cancer you should hope to get if you had a choice.' If I had a choice, I wouldn't have it, and if I had to have it, I'd want surgery and be done with it. But I didn't get a choice. I saw the fight I was about to go through for the next six months, and had to cross my fingers and hope this treatment would work. My life was being handed over to chemo.

We didn't have to wait long, much to my disappointment. The chemo nurse showed me to my seat, and I looked around and watched what everyone else was doing.

I have cancer and I'm getting chemotherapy . . . I have cancer and I'm getting chemotherapy.

That just kept going on and on in my head, until I burst into tears again. The nurse came over to me, and I apologised over and over, incredibly embarrassed for acting like an idiot. She smiled and comforted me straight away, telling me it was absolutely normal. Really? It was normal to cry like this? So how come no one else was in tears?

Before being hooked in to anything, I went to the toilet and pushed the last of my tears out. I wanted to get the crying under control and out of the way. I looked in the mirror, shook my head at myself, unhappy with how I'd reacted all morning and feeling like a moron (normal or not), and told myself to suck it up. I had to make a commitment to myself to get through the next six months of my life, *for* my life.

I walked back out, sat in the chair, smiled at Paul, and I was ready. The nurse talked me through the procedure of how chemo is administered. I was to have four treatment bags, each ranging in the type of drug, duration of injection, symptoms and side effects. She asked me a range of questions and told me the results of my blood test results.

My haemoglobin (the protein in the red blood cells), were at a good level of 125 (the normal levels being from 115-165). When red blood cell counts are too low, chemo cannot be given. Blood transfusions are normal throughout treatment, as the chemotherapy wipes blood cells, which may cause mild anaemia.

I had my blood pressure checked and my body temperature checked, and I was good to go. We asked her how long treatment lasts, and she told us that, depending on how my body reacted and my veins coped with the last bag, it could be anywhere from four to six hours.

She brought over a tub of warm water to soak my hand, to help the vein open up ready for the needle and the cannula. The chemo is given through an IV, with saline solution in between bags of treatment, to help flush the drug through the bloodstream. Sounded simple.

While I sat there with my hand soaking, I began pitifully lamenting my former life. Paul looked at me and told me something that fired up my strength. 'Karina, think of it this way: you're on the first step of a ladder. After today, you'll only have eleven more steps to go. You're getting closer to the end with each treatment. You know you can do this.'

Remembering what the oncologist said to me about lymphoma patients looking forward to their chemo, I found my determination again.

The long list of symptoms I had now was embedded in my brain. Living with them all, day in day out, I was drained from thinking of them all.

I couldn't remember what life was like pre symptoms, and I couldn't wait to find out. The nurse came back and found a vein she was happy with and injected the cannula that was to be used during treatment. She gave me an anti-vomiting tablet (Emend), another called Ondansetron, a steroid injection (Dexamethosone) to counteract inflammation, nausea and vomiting, an anti-nausea tablet (Pramin), and paracetamol.

Here we go. It was going to be a long day.

I looked around and saw that every single chair in the ward was occupied, with more patients upstairs. Far out. How many people does this affect? So many faces, some lying in the beds, too weak to sit up; some getting blood transfusions behind curtains; some in wheelchairs:

and some privately vomiting, pale, gaunt and weak. I wanted to go to them and hug them all, tell them I was there for them and that I understood some of what they were going through.

I felt so sorry seeing all these people, especially the patients in their beds. I had to fight back my tears again. This was all blatantly wrong. No part of cancer is fair for any one of us, especially for the innocent children battling in the wards above us. How can that be justified?

The nurse explained that the three or four days following treatment would be the hardest; when the nausea, possible vomiting, diarrhoea, and general feeling like crap would be at its peak. Something to look forward to, but I was thankful for the heads up.

I was given a special card that had listed all the chemo drugs I was being given. This card would allow me urgent attention if I ended up in hospital, like a VIP. We are very lucky in this country to have a system like this in place.

The nurse hooked me up to a saline bag to flush my bloodstream. When the saline was empty she came over in a protective gown and gloves with my first chemo bag. Why so much protection, I thought. I had to ask her, I couldn't help myself. She explained that because chemo is toxic, they had to protect themselves from any splashes or spills. Oh yeah, okay . . . I think.

The nurse connected the bag, started the chemo through the pump, and reminded me to be aware of any strange feelings or dizziness. I didn't expect chemo to be like this.

She went to attend to another patient and Paul and I were left alone. I concentrated hard on how I was feeling until the bag was drained of the drug it was holding. Nope, didn't feel any different. Is this it? Did I cry all morning for this? Oh, didn't I feel totally stupid.

The patient's husband next to us introduced himself and we started having a conversation. He had overheard how I'd asked the nurse why they had to be so protected with gloves and gowns, so he chose that moment to tell me, 'Chemo is really poison, you know. Some of them in the past were used as insecticides. They even cause different types of cancer in other parts of the body, even while killing the one it's meant for. Secondary cancers. You heard of those? I don't know how the government allows these drugs to be given to people like this. With all the money raised for all the different cancer organisations in the world, you'd think they would have come up with a better solution by now.'

I didn't know whether to brush it off or cry. Toxic poisons? So that's what was going in my body? That was the only answer we had in the world? Where does all the money go, then?

After speaking with this man and meeting others during the day, I understood quickly that everyone in the ward had different opinions about their cancer journey. Some patients, and supporters, were still angry. Others were confused. But most had learnt that this was a new way of life, and fought with acceptance, because what else was there?

It was essential for my own sanity not to take everything people would say to me seriously, or personally. Everyone was at different stages of their journey, and processed things differently, unique to our own experiences, emotions and beliefs. Still, there was a unity and familiarity between us all, like we belonged together, and understood each other, offering some form of comfort and inspiration to fight.

The nurse came over and asked me how I was feeling. Satisfied that I was okay, she hooked up the saline, and the second chemo bag followed. Here we go again. Only two more bags to go! The second bag went in smoothly, both of them in under twenty minutes.

Oh, Karina, you idiot. I'd been hysterical for nothing!

In the research I'd done, I'd come across an interview with Olivia Newton John. She had spoken about her own experience with breast cancer and chemo, where she would visualise her chemo as a stream of pure gold liquid going into her body to heal her, rather than the poison that it is.

So as the third bag started flowing into my vein, I did the same, conscious of my own strength. This bag of chemo drained for longer than the first two, but it was easy. I was up to the last bag and I was so proud of myself that it was nearly over. When the nurse came over with the last bag, she explained that this one was known to cause slight vein irritation and possible burning, so it was to be administered slower than the first three. This one could take roughly an hour or two.

Pfft, it won't bother me, I thought. I've had three bags, what's one more? I would just visualise the chemo as liquid gold again.

I spoke too soon.

Hooking my IV to the last bag, the look of it scared me half to death. In front of me was a full bag with a black cover over it to protect it from light. It was a big black, ugly, demonic-looking bag. Oh no.

The infusion started slowly and I didn't feel anything, so she increased it. It felt okay, so I told her to try it with a faster flow. I was so over it already and I just wanted to go home. She set it up and went to check on other patients.

That's when I started to feel a mild icy sting in my hand that crawled up through my forearm to my upper arm, and around my shoulder. At first I could handle it. Breathe through it, Karina, I told myself. I can so do this. It doesn't hurt, it doesn't hurt.

Jolting me out of my affirmations, the icy sting quickly turning into a blaze of scorching fire through my arm!

'Paul! Get the nurse! *Please!*' I was desperate for it to stop. With each second that passed I felt like I was being incinerated on the inside! My hand started shaking from the pain and I jumped up into my chair with the desperation to do something! Make it stop, make it stop! I was pleading with no one but myself!

My heart pounded as time stood still! The spreading lava in my veins was incinerating my entire arm! I squeezed my eyes shut trying to block it out and held my breath, as my body broke into a heated sweat.

I could hear the nurse running over to me, and she immediately stopped the flow. She raced over and put a wheat pack in the microwave to warm up the vein and relieve the pain. As soon as she placed it on my arm, the immense relief was breathtaking.

The pressure that had been building and thumping through my head from that sudden onset of agony lifted instantly. I could breathe again. She wasn't kidding when she said this bag could cause slight irritation, although 'slight' was a severe understatement.

Once I'd recovered, she tried the flow again. I cringed in my chair, shut my eyes and squeezed Paul's hand. I couldn't leave without having it. With my wheat pack on and a slower flow, I ignored the stinging to get it over with as quickly as possible. Keeping my eyes tight shut, I tried to daydream that I was anywhere but there.

Half way through the bag, I began feeling symptoms.

My heart started racing and it became hard to breathe. Am I having a panic attack? I tried to remember what I'd been thinking about, but nothing in my head was that bad, was it? Then I became edgy, grinding my teeth and wanting to burst out of there and run! Wanting to rip out the cables, I grabbed the pole the IV was hooked to, and walked back and forth towards the toilet, trying to calm myself down taking as many slow shallow breaths as I could.

Finally going into the lavatory, I held my breath again and I focused on the sweet relief of peeing. Lucky she had warned me that the colour of pee changes to a bright red because of the chemo. It looked like blood, which would horrify anyone without pre warning.

I looked in the mirror and my swollen face was turning an awful shade of yellow. The circles under my eyes had darkened and were sunken. My body was slightly desensitised with tingling down my arms and legs. I told the sallow reflection to keep going. 'You can do this, Karina. You've been through so much already in this life, this is just one more thing. Don't give up now. You're stronger than that.'

I needed to get out of there. It was late and I wanted to go home.

It took over five hours for that bag to drain entirely. I'd been in the hospital from 10:30 that morning and we finally finished at 6pm. What a long day. Thank god for my girlfriends.

One in particular, Bec, never let me down, offering to pick up my kids from school so I wouldn't have to worry about rushing back without finishing treatment, and she would continue to do so every fortnight through the entire six months. My children had their own safe house where they could be themselves among other kids.

Exhausted from the emotions and anxiety of the morning, and the physical fatigue of having chemo, it was a consolation to know that my kids were in a safe place, having fun, and happy.

And I did it. I survived my first day and was pretty damn proud of myself.

The nurses reminded us that if I did throw up at home, we had to wear gloves when cleaning up and disinfect the toilet to protect the rest of the family. That bothered me. How bad is this stuff then?

We collected all the medication necessary to get through the following three days—more of my golden sparkly Oxycontin—and we left. One down, eleven more to go. It wasn't that bad. I could get through the next six months, easy.

With the last bag of chemo, I was convinced that I would never be able to drive myself home after treatment. My reflexes were slow, my vision was foggy, and I was delirious and dizzy with a heavy rock of nausea in my gut.

Once we were home, I went downhill quickly. I began to feel weak and extremely tired. My head felt detached from the rest of me, while my stomach was heavy with piercing jabs of colic. My body became hot and clammy with the intense waves of nausea, but taking the anti-nausea medication would calm it down.

I had to run to the toilet several times with a severe case of burning diarrhoea, which was okay with me. My body was clearly trying to purge itself from the chemo, so I was happy to go as many times as possible. In between the toilet runs, I'd lie on the couch with my eyes closed and listen to my family talk about their day. Listening to my kids' voices was soothing and music to my ears. Content that I had got through the first treatment, I didn't care about any of the chemo symptoms. I was finally on the road to recovery.

That night I had a blissful sleep, even through the strong waves of nausea that would waken me every couple of hours with the usual body aches and sweats. As long as I kept taking the medications, I was in my happy place.

11

LIVING IN THE LIGHT

Treatment one

The first day following chemo I woke up feeling fairly normal, besides the disturbed sleep of waking up every couple of hours to pee.

The nausea rising from the middle of my throat and the burning reflux would wretch my stomach, and I quickly fell in love with all the anti-vomiting and anti-nausea drugs.

My medication schedule and all the boxes of tablets were mind-boggling.

Day one of chemotherapy

- Emend x1 tablet (anti-vomiting—one hour before treatment)
- Ondansetron x1 (anti-vomiting—prior to chemo)
- Dexamethasone (anti-inflammatory steroid—prior to chemo)

Day two

Emend x1 tablet before breakfast

Day three

Emend x1 tablet before breakfast

Every day

- Progout (anti-gout treatment) x1 tab every day for the first 30 days
- Stemzine® (anti-nausea) 2 tablets x3 times daily (or when required)
- Pramin (anti-nausea) 2 tablets x3 times daily
- Somac® (for reflux) when required
- Gastro-stop (only in the case of diarrhoea)
- Movicol® and Coloxyl® Senna laxatives

Besides all of those medications, I was still taking my usual pain relief of Oxycontin, Tramadol and Paracetamol.

I was a walking pharmacy.

The hunger that ravaged through the nausea was unbelievable. How I could be ravenous while having severe nausea and acid build up in the gut, was beyond me. The steroid.

I wanted to be a kickass chemo patient. No more crying or whingeing, no more questioning, no getting sick. Adamant to stay completely normal, I decided that I would just keep going on with my days—my usual routine of family and friends.

Despite looking yellow and swollen, and feeling horrible on the inside, it was an uneventful day. As long as I remembered my medication every three to four hours, I was as comfortable as I could be—pain free and sick free.

Throughout the day tiredness would slowly creep up on me. Dry retching from the thick nausea would involuntarily contract my stomach muscles. I'd been living with so many symptoms for so long then that these new symptoms simply became something interesting and different to live with. I was used to things changing inside me on a daily basis.

My kids and my typical mum routine helped to distract me. I didn't have much time to think about anything. I still had to get up early and get my kids to school, and, as hard as it was, that's what helped me and the rest of my family stay sane.

To help my children ease into this transition, I informed their teachers of what our family were about to endure for the next six months. I asked them to keep an eye on my girls, in case they found it difficult to adjust, and to simply support them as much as possible. I needed to help my kids comfortably slide into this new world of cancer and chemo . . . in every aspect of their world.

On day four I plunged into the darkness of chemotherapy. The 'dark day.' That day all blood cells were wiped from my body, trapping me with fatigue, weakness and depression.

Even though the sky was beautifully blue and cloudless, everything looked overcast to me. A veil of darkness shrouded any light, as if I were looking through dark tinted glass. I couldn't smile. I couldn't laugh or talk, and my head was heavy with frustration and sorrow.

I rushed my kids to school that morning so they wouldn't have to see me like that. I wanted to hide from everything and everyone; to hide from the world. I realised it was the dark day the nurses had warned me about, but I never imagined it would be as heavy as this.

I switched the phones off and lay on the couch. No TV, no sounds, just mind-numbing silence. The day painfully crawled on, as a dark cloud hung over my head, squeezing out any joy for life I had. Caught in the most intense sadness I had ever known, I felt myself go under with no control. When I thought of the six months of treatment the end of it seemed far away, like a six-month prison sentence. I was being punished, held a prisoner to my own body, with the waiting and hoping to be free of cancer my prosecution.

What if I go through the next six months of chemo for nothing? What if it doesn't work? I considered giving up, never having chemo again, stopping my treatment and just letting the cancer take me. Maybe I deserved to die? Maybe I was a bad person and this was meant to be. Who was I to stop it? I'm nothing.

And then I would have to wait another eleven years, shackled to a ball and chain by cancer, just to be 'safe' from disease. I did this to myself. I must have.

Those were my morbid thoughts as I slid into an all-consuming pit. This dark day was messing with my head and I couldn't wait for it to be over. It was hopeless. I was falling in its grasp, but I was so far from caring about anything that I let it take me.

I went outside and sat in the sun, hoping to free myself from the shadows. Even the sunshine was clouded in a haze of darkness. There was a bottomless void deep inside my being, creating a confusing emptiness so far out of reach that I felt nothing. It didn't make a difference what I did. I was tired, cornered and powerless.

Please, stop! I tried clearing my mind and being positive, being grateful for my family and the support I had around me, but it didn't work and I couldn't understand it?

I turned away from the darkness, trying harder to snap out of it, telling myself to shut up, but I was exhausted. This wasn't worth it. Nothing was worth fighting for anymore. I hated the world and everyone in it. Life had been a bitch to me for far too long.

That thought infuriated me because I knew it was rubbish. I had many blessings and a family to be grateful for. There were beautiful people surrounding me, so why was I so intent on fixating on the crap?

Exploding with guilt, I was disgusted at being defeated by my own mind. This wasn't like me. I pushed myself to think of my kids again, and of Paul, but I was blinded by this nightmare that I couldn't get out of, possessed by a dominating evil force.

My body weighed a million tons as I hit a dead end. As much as it was hard to accept, I couldn't fight it anymore and ended up rationalising the bleakness. As much as I hated the negative feelings and emotions, I accepted them, surrendering to my own mind. As I did, it became easier to deal with.

That night I went to bed early, looking forward to a different day. I didn't want to tell my family how I was feeling as it would hurt them, or hurt me to realise that they couldn't understand me. I was scared that my own family would think I was insane.

Waking up the next day, I opened my eyes and lay still, searching my mind for any hint of darkness. But it was over. I had finally woken up from the ordeal of the day before.

I grabbed my kids and kissed them a million times until they'd had enough. Welcome back, Karina.

After dropping the kids at school I sat down recalling the day before. I now had first-hand experience of what to expect if it ever happened again and I was kind of grateful to have had it so early in my journey—now I was armed and ready for the next one.

Overwhelmed with guilt as I remembered the thoughts and emotions of the day before, of the hatred above all else, I became so angry for allowing my mind to go down that path, but it had been out of my hands. The darkness had been stronger than me, and now all that was left to do, was forgive myself, and let it go.

I was aware that this was all part of the roller coaster of having cancer and going through treatment. This is what the hospital staff try to warn of. Maybe I should see a counsellor, I thought, but I'm not crazy. A counsellor wouldn't understand. No one would understand, and I'd probably end up on more medication for some severe mental disorder.

I couldn't bear the thought of telling anyone what I'd experienced and decided to deal with it on my own, empowering me that much more.

Feeling around my mouth with my tongue, a few painful mouth sores had ruptured. My stomach was on fire with reflux through the nausea, so I washed my mouth out with warm salty water, hoping this was all a means to an end.

Nothing and no one was going to stop me from getting my life back again, from being free. Belief and trust in myself began to bloom. I didn't care about the chemo symptoms because I saw the end of it. I *would* overthrow cancer—that was my mantra.

The following week Dr Louis Cali called me to collect my herbs. I was really looking forward to starting them, hoping that they would help me with my symptoms.

Seeing Dr Cali would change the rest of my journey.

Once he finished explaining the herbs to me, he examined my eyes and searched around my face, checked my tongue and felt my pulse in both wrists. Well, this was different. When he finished examining me and noting his findings on paper, we started the acupuncture.

According to Dr Cali, treatment with acupuncture often gives patients a deep sense of well-being—it takes tension and stress out of the system. This can be both physical and mental stress. Patients consistently report that they feel more relaxed and at ease after a treatment. Keeping body and mind strong during a battle with cancer is an important part of a patient's journey. Remembering the stress of the dark day, I was really looking forward to this.

After a couple of minutes listening to the soothing music, and feeling like a porcupine, I wondered whether all this stuff would work. Was I wasting my time? Try anything, I told myself. As if to answer my own questions, the bed started to spin. At first it was a gentle spin. I could handle that. It was kind of fun and weird when I'd open my eyes to see that nothing was moving. This was definitely in my head. Then the gentle spin turned into a whirlpool, like being flushed down a turbo jet toilet.

I gripped the sides of the bed, scared that I would fly off, and opened my eyes again. The bed was still in the same position, but the room was spinning so fast! My body would sway towards the edge of the bed, and I'd quickly hold on to stop myself from falling, while realising that I hadn't moved so much as an inch.

I tried concentrating on the traffic noises outside on the main road to no avail. I kept spinning faster and faster, catapulting upwards only to come crashing back down again, in a series of waves and surges. My legs felt like they were lifting off from the centrifugal force. I swear all I could picture was a gigantic washing machine hauling me through a spin cycle! Just then Dr Cali came in to check on me. I told him about the spinning and he told me that the chemo treatment throws the body out of balance and my body was now returning to its normal balance. Far out!

I wanted to do this more than ever. With the reaction I was having, I was confident that this was working. After a few more minutes, just as I started getting used to the sensation, it stopped.

Unfortunately, this was the only acupuncture treatment that had me spinning. In the following six months, I looked forward to more internal joy rides, but it seemed that the first one had the most powerful effect.

The next morning, I had no choice but to use another enema. The laxatives were doing absolutely nothing to help the blockaded bowel movements and I really hoped the herbs would help in that department.

Taking the herbal remedy was vile, with a strong and bitter repulsive taste but I preferred that compared to any more enemas. The putrid smell of the herbs mixing with the boiled water revolted me. It took all my willpower to drink the concoction.

As a precaution, I took my anti-nausea pills again and waited for my stomach to settle. Once it was safe, I brought the mug up to my mouth to try to drink the tea, and I managed to get in about half a mouthful. That was enough to start me retching. How was I expected to drink this stuff?

I ran to the bathroom in case I vomited, and tried again. Looking in the mirror, I saw my horrified expression and had to laugh at myself. I saw the dark circles under my eyes and the sallow colour of my face and I knew I needed it. Telling myself why I had to do this, that I could do *anything*, I made myself down the entire cupful without breathing and mentally switched off my taste buds. Ugh!

12

THROUGH THE FOG

Treatments two to four

It's true what they say: the first few treatments are the easiest. Well, as easy as chemo gets. In hindsight, it really wasn't that bad, particularly the first two treatments. They were, without question, the easiest. I was eternally grateful that I had not experienced another dark day.

The stomach cramps and ongoing nausea were more annoying than difficult to live with. It was like pregnancy with all day morning sickness, but as long as I remembered to take my new loves, Pramin and my herbal formulae, I was okay. I absolutely hate throwing up.

I could feel the herbal formulae helping to support my body, as the mouth ulcers cleared up, the acidity in my stomach slowly dissipated, and, best of all, my bowels began moving daily. Thankfully, I hadn't looked at another laxative or enema.

The first four or five days straight after chemo were strange and the most difficult. It was an odd sensation of not being in my body, or not knowing my body. A part of me felt detached, as if I was walking on the inside of a gigantic air bubble. Of course, in my head I knew where I was, but I wasn't physically quite *in* my body.

I'd have to watch what I ate in the first week after treatments. I would stick to fresh vegetable juices and fruits, crackers and toast. It's not that I wasn't hungry, I definitely was. But I guess I was too scared to eat anything that could trigger vomiting, and the nausea put me off heavy food.

Aside from loading myself with watermelon to quench my thirst, water bottles, warm thick socks and magazines, I'd take a DVD into the chemo ward and watch it on the hospital's portable DVD players. Completely losing myself into the movie I was watching, I was on a sort of mini holiday with my own 'hotel' staff waiting on me. As dubious as it sounds, I actually looked forward to treatments. I looked forward to being in a room full of people that were, to some degree, on the same level as me.

We would always exchange sincere smiles, and acknowledge each other with a genuine wink or a nod that only we understood. There was a mutual unspoken respect and I was so proud of us. Chemo was a place where we weren't divided by different coloured ribbons, or segregated into different groups. We were in there for the same reason: to obliterate cancer. We were one.

One patient had been having chemo treatments for three years, on a four weekly basis. Her name was Amy.

Her treatment was designed to hinder the growth of the tumour in her bowel, as her type of cancer couldn't be eradicated. She was a naturopath and had been extremely healthy, a non-smoker, yet cancer had made its way in her body. Unbelievable. That's when I stopped seeing my own cancer as a personal attack.

Amy told me that she'd had regular colonics before being diagnosed with bowel cancer, but she had worked through her guilt because chemo had become her new way of life. She was so happy to be there, to be alive, and I truly admired her.

When I mentioned my admiration, she stopped me in my tracks, shrugged it off, and told me that I was in there doing the same as her, and having treatment for the same reason. She urged me to acknowledge and admire myself for what I was going through and to recognise my own strength. Her attitude was, 'You do what you have to do, right?' and I couldn't have agreed more.

Other patients I spoke with were still confused. 'Why?' was the biggest question for everyone. Some were like me, first time cancer patients. Some were revisiting alternative chemo treatments after relapsing, trying different regimes and drugs. It didn't matter, young or old, healthy or not, smoker or non-smoker.

A glimpse into a grim reality of what others live through daily was a wake up call to appreciate my own battle, especially when I saw teenagers in the ward, and knowing children as young as eight months old were fighting their own disease in the levels above us. A gross injustice of this world.

During treatment number three (four weeks into treatment), something happened that shook my foundations and opened my eyes to what chemo is all about.

While soaking my hands in the tub of warm water for my veins to be better hijacked, I joked with one of the nurses in there, Carmen, about ordering a flat screen TV and having a beautiful view of the ocean (which was really a rusting balcony overlooking scrub and trees and an old parking lot).

We'd joke about room service and I'd 'order' my chemo cocktail with 'a hint of vodka and tequila' in it. It was nice to be able to bring some humour into that place, even if I was only amusing myself. And it was equally refreshing that she would go along with me.

The nurse that was administering my chemo that day was having trouble injecting my vein, as they were on the verge of collapse. Already? Oh terrific! I didn't care how long it took her to find a vein, I wanted my chemo and I wasn't leaving without it.

Finally, after a few painful jabs, she found a vein, and hooked me up to my usual cocktail. The other patients had PICC lines on their chests or in their arms and I wanted one too. It looked so much easier to deal with.

Across from me, one of the patients started complaining to the nurses that he was feeling light headed. His face turned a mean shade of purple and he started shivering uncontrollably. All we could do was stare. I didn't mean to be rude, but I was desperate for him to get some help.

He began violently convulsing. In what seemed like half a second, he had about four or five nurses around him. This all happened so quickly I couldn't believe what I was seeing.

They injected something into his PICC line, and he fell asleep. Gradually his colour started coming back to his face and his fingers. They had a heap of heated blankets on him, and that's when the true meaning of chemotherapy hit me. The realness of it. I wanted to get up from my city of pillows and break into a standing ovation for the team of nurses. What they did was remarkable! To witness the urgency from every one of them to help this man was astounding. My respect for nurses everywhere amplified.

Speaking with the man later in the afternoon, he explained that he'd had an allergic reaction to his chemo. I didn't even know that was possible. He began telling us that this was his third relapse with his type of cancer, and each time they would have to stop his treatments due to similar reactions triggered by his diabetes and a dangerously low blood pressure. He knew his chances for survival were slim while they searched for an appropriate treatment regime, yet he was strong and positive, another inspiring fighter.

The last bag of chemo, the black, scary-as-hell, demonic looking thing, was my worst enemy. I hated it.

It would burn through my veins, and then turn me into a light-headed zombie with strong nausea, dizziness, heart palpitations and fierce anxiety attacks.

Near the end of a chemo day, my stomach seemed to grow cement blocks that would rise up into my throat. Nausea would erupt, but would easily settle again with medication. My treatments lasted just over eight hours. All I wanted was to be home around my kids.

As my veins were on the verge of collapse, I asked for a PICC line, and I was given an appointment time for the following week. No more needles!

On our way out, I gave the pharmacist the list of ingredients in my herbal formulae, and, as expected, I was told to immediately cease taking them, as they would counteract the chemo. Did I listen? No.

I followed my instinct and Dr Cali's advice.

It so happened that Blackstreet, Paul's favourite group of our old school R&B days, came into town that same weekend. Exhausted from having chemo just two days earlier, I went along anyway. It was part of 'keeping my normal routine' plan. Paul's dream was coming true. He was going to meet his idol, Teddy Riley. I had to be there to see his face and share in that moment.

It was one of the best concerts I had been to, but standing for hours in the queue and then during the show took a toll on my body. I really should have been in bed.

Throughout the show, my hands and arms would tingle down to my fingers, and my knees locked into a stiff position as the pain in my chest started its mild infiltration. In the middle of the crowd, I frantically took my Oxycontin and anti-nausea meds, as the heavy dry heaving began. I was calling the shots, not the cancer, and I was adamant that I would have a good night, whatever it took, for Paul. If anything, I wanted to create these good memories, just in case something did happen to me.

I watched these grown men morph into high-pitched screaming fans, as everyone around me began singing and dancing, and wished I could be like them. Normal. Not to have to go through chemo and PET scans, and blood tests, and hospital visits—to be able to dance freely without a care in the world. My greatest love has always been dancing, and my childhood passion was to be a dancer.

I dreamt of being on stage again as I did when I was younger, letting the music and movements take me to another dimension, getting lost in the moment. The dance floor is a place that knows no bounds or stress. I closed my eyes and felt the beat, the bass, the melody, and let it all take me.

Even through the pain in my legs and the aches in my chest, I didn't want it to end. When it did, we had more long hours of waiting ahead of us to meet the band.

It was past midnight and we had been there from 5pm. Seeing the line growing at the meet and greet area, I asked for a chair, dying to sit down. Urgently wanting to go home sooner rather than later, I mentioned that I'd had chemo a couple of days earlier and the exhaustion of that mixed with the adrenaline of the concert was wearing me down.

As much as I didn't like seeing the hasty and sympathetic reaction to the words 'cancer' and 'chemo,' we were immediately bumped up to the front of the line to meet Teddy Riley and the other band members.

Cancer had given me a power that I didn't necessarily want or like, but I wanted my bed as soon as possible and more pain relief. My whole body was throbbing. And it was cool to have Teddy Riley say a quick heartfelt prayer for my recovery. Very cool.

The following week I went to get my PICC line inserted. It was a very basic and easy procedure. The doctor came in, checked the veins in the inside of my upper arm through an ultra sound. He anesthetised the area, made a small incision through the skin, and inserted a tube into the vein and fed it through until it was in the blood vessel near my heart. And that was it. All up it took about half an hour. Well, that was cool! I felt really special with my PICC. It was my medal of honour—my ally in the fight to win.

When the local anaesthetic wore off, I had slight stinging from the cut, but it was nothing compared to the raw surgery wound still healing in my chest. I had to keep an eye on that wound and the bleeding since my platelet levels were low from chemo, but apart from that everything was fine.

My GP clinic would help me take care of the PICC line incision area, cleaning it and watching for infections over the following months, as well as the surgery wound in my chest. I loved my doctors and nurses and appreciated them so much. Dr Raj, Daniela and the entire team were extremely supportive. Things would have been very different if I hadn't had such a great support team behind me.

After the third treatment I was almost feeling pre symptoms again! The lymphoma symptoms had decreased substantially. I could swallow real food again. I could talk and laugh without going into coughing fits. My heart didn't palpitate as much, and I was sleeping better during the night. I could sneeze and yawn without bracing myself. I could take a deep breath, and the best part—no more night sweats and chills. I finally started feeling good again. It must be working.

Yes, chemo was definitely worth it.

I found that I didn't need to take the anti-vomiting medication. The Chinese herbal formulae were helping. Physically, I felt the difference from the first treatment to the third one. My energy levels had increased slightly. I was generally happier and felt stronger and healthier.

My digestive issues with the acidity, mouth sores, diarrhoea and constipation were things of the past. I slowly began weaning myself off the Oxycontin, and it worked! No more excruciating upper body aches and pains that a simple Tramadol couldn't handle! That was the best part. I felt good. The anti-nausea meds were all I needed.

Although I was feeling the healing effects of the chemo and Chinese medicine, I was still worried when I went for my first PET scan just before the fourth treatment. There was the slight possibility that the tumour hadn't reduced in size, or worse, had grown instead. Truthfully, I was scared as hell.

The following week, week while waiting for the results, life went on as usual. My new shiny PICC line was used at my fourth chemo treatment. It was awesome to watch them simply plug in under my arm. There was no jabbing or piercing pain, and the best part was that I was freed from the searing veins the demonic bag produced. I loved my PICC line and I was convinced that chemo would be a breeze from then on, although I still turned into a semi-comatose, anxiety-wracked zombie by the end of a treatment day.

I went to see my new doctor, Dr Stephen Opat, the following week for the results of the PET scan. As he read through the results, I watched his face carefully. He kept reading, I kept studying.

Chill, Karina. Let the man read the results.

Come on, come on, come on, come on!

Rigorously twisting my fingers in the stress of waiting and cracking all of my knuckles, I couldn't take the suspense any more. Finally, after a million minutes, he looked at me and said, 'Well, it seems that you're in remission, Karina. Congratulations.'

Huh? What? He smiled at me and waited for the information to sink in. 'It looks like your tumour has reduced quite significantly in size. It's just under half the size from when you started treatment, so this tells us that the chemo is working. The cancer is responding successfully to the ABVD and you can continue treatment until the twelve treatments are finished. In fact, the tumour has reduced in size quite remarkably. We usually expect a good response with Hodgkins and ABVD, and this response has been fast.'

My grin stretched from ear to ear. It was working! Not only was the chemo working, but the *herbs were working*! The herbs hadn't counteracted the chemo! I wanted to kiss him!

I excused myself fast and power walked out of there. I had to get onto the phone—I called Paul first and told him the news. As soon as I told him, I could hear the relief in his voice.

We were both laughing and crying and I was trying to balance my phone while wiping my nose. I started jumping up and down yelling into the phone, 'It's working, baby! It's working!'

I could hear his smile from my end. 'See Karina? Sex works! It fixes everything.'

Typical Paul. I burst into tears from laughter.

Telling my dad was amazing. I was so happy to finally give him some good news; something good to think about. This was my dad. My rock.

To hear him crying with joy and relief was one of the most beautiful and precious moments of my life.

'Call your mother, call your mother!' he urged.

She reacted the same way, screaming at the top of her lungs to anyone and everyone who was listening at work, 'It's working, it's working! The tumour is shrinking! The bastard tumour is dying! Ding dong, the bitch is dead!' Well, forget the tears! I snorted and broke into a fit of laughter. 'Yeah, Karina! You did it, you did it! And those herbs helped you kick it in the arse!'

I couldn't stop crying and laughing and snorting.

Happiness spread through my heart like wild fire! I wanted to skip out of there, run so fast, jump up and down and scream!

Hang on. You still have to get through the next eight treatments.

That was the logical side of my brain trying to squash my joy, but I didn't think twice about it. I was happy! And I wanted to sit in this happy place for the next few days.

On my way home, the radio station must have been in sync with my moment, because *I'm A Survivor* by Destiny's Child came on. I turned up that song and fist pumped a few times, screaming the lyrics at the top of my lungs to the shrivelling tumour, tears of pride streaming down my face! I didn't care that the drivers in other cars were staring at me as if I were crazy. Because I was!

Treatments five and six

By the fifth chemo treatment, I was surprised at how manageable chemo seemed. Besides the arduous first week, it wasn't such a big deal and I wondered what the hype was all about. The only downside was that just when I'd start to feel good for a few days, I'd have another treatment and feel the thick, nauseated, dizziness, and weirdness again. However, once those symptoms subsided, only mild tiredness weighed me down.

By the second week of treatment I was almost back to my normal self. I loved my herbal formulae.

Frustrated with hibernating on my own at home, I'd escape to Mel's home. Hers was a house where I could be totally normal, without a smidgen of special care. I was tired of being treated like a fragile vase about to break.

I noticed people began changing around me. They would either apologise during normal conversations about something positive happening in their lives, or just blatantly avoid me. So, when things became too serious, I'd take refuge at Mel's. We would spend the day together laughing and talking about everything but cancer. It was perfect. When I wasn't at Mel's, I'd go to Tracy's, my second escape house, for movie marathons and time out. Patrick Swayze and Dirty Dancing . . . what a distraction. Tracy knew exactly what I needed.

Being a typical woman, one of the side effects of chemo that I was most fearful of was losing my long hair. By treatment five, the physical changes I dreaded descended at colossal speeds.

The top of my head had been sensitive in the days leading up to treatment five due to inflammation of my hair follicles. It felt like permanent bruising. However, after treatment five, my scalp became extremely sensitive, burning with a smouldering heat that would last about a week after treatment.

During this time, I was petrified of washing my hair. I'd stand under cold running water to relieve my scalp from the heat. After building up the courage to gently massage shampoo through it, I found that it wasn't that bad to touch. But rinsing the shampoo, my hair became a tangled mess in my hands. I looked down to see clumps of hair being washed towards the drain. My hair was melting off my head. Awe, shock and revulsion hit the pit of my stomach in waves.

Falling to my knees onto the shower floor, I erupted into a torrent of tears and sobs. *No! Not my hair!* I dismally stared at it as it gathered into a gigantic pile. Even though I knew this hair loss came hand in hand with chemo, I was shattered.

I was going to be this ugly, hairless, sick person. I was going to *look* like a cancer patient. Images of cartoon witches with warts on their noses and bald patches on their heads blasted into my imagination. That's what I'm going to look like.

My self-esteem hit the floor. I didn't feel like a woman anymore. I was losing my femininity.

I remembered the girl in the waiting room wearing the wig and how I'd thought I would be immune to hair loss and it wouldn't affect me—what a big mistake.

Paul caught me as I came out of the shower. I burst into tears, almost expecting him to fall out of love with me at that moment. He reassured me an infinite amount of times of his love for me and that, in his eyes, I was the most beautiful woman in the world. That's a very hard compliment to believe when you don't believe it yourself.

Then he told me to save some hair for him so he could cover his bald patch. He accused me of wanting to look like him—bald with hairy legs. I cracked up laughing. I now have a new found sympathy to all men who have lost their hair.

Sadly, losing hair was to become another norm and another issue to live with, happening at every hair wash and in between washes. I would walk around the house, run my fingers through my hair and end up with clumps of it twisted around my fingers and mountains of it in my hands. It became so brittle and tangled that, coupled with the scalp pain, it was hard to get a comb through it.

So Tracy cut it short for me, spoiling me with intense conditioning treatments thereafter, and it became easier to manage.

My eyelashes began falling out and disappearing just as fast as my hair. That was probably harder to deal with than losing the hair on my head. Eyeliner just didn't look the same and mascara would clump on the two or three strands of eyelashes that were left standing.

They say the only relief from the burning chemo scalp and hair loss is to shave it, but I couldn't bring myself to do that. Not yet. The Leukaemia Foundation had been advertising The World's Greatest Shave that would happen in two months' time, so I signed up and registered to shave my head. It was better to shave it while raising money for the foundation—that way losing my hair wasn't a total loss and I'd kill two birds with one stone.

While I was losing hair on my head, it would've been extremely convenient and a much better alternative to lose it on other parts of my body instead. Not having to shave or wax would be every woman's dream!

Basically, I had to get rid of the jungle of hair growing everywhere else, and decided to go against all the warnings from the hospital staff and shave my legs. If I did it carefully, who would notice? I just had to try not to cut myself . . . and I know I'm not the only patient that has gone and done this.

While shaving, I noticed a few bruises on my legs and, as I don't normally bruise easily, it intrigued me to see them. Oh well. Something else to get used to.

I did end up cutting myself, and the amount of watery blood gushing out of the cut was amazing. I've never seen anything like it. The platelet levels in my bloodstream were clearly low, and it took almost an hour for the small shaving cut to stop bleeding. The harrowing part about that was knowing that the chemo was absolutely and unmistakably affecting my body internally, while it was killing the mass of cancer.

The day before going in for treatment six, I went in to have the routine blood tests. These tests are done fortnightly before each treatment to ensure the blood cell count is gradually increasing and recovering lost cells. If the cell count is too low, chemo is postponed until the levels recover.

During this blood test, the pain of the needle piercing my skin stunned me breathless—since when did blood tests become so painful? It was unnerving. All the simple and small things I was so used to were radically changing and becoming harder to deal with.

However, weighing the good with the bad, these small changes were worth it if it meant living without lymphoma.

After treatment six, the first few days were little harder than after the previous treatments, and at the same time a little easier because I was knew what to expect.

I began losing my sense of taste and smell, mainly in the first week after treatment. Having food on my tongue but only feeling its texture in my mouth, was a very awkward sensation, and frustrating, because I love food. The strong taste and sweetness of chocolate would only slightly break through the tasteless barrier.

Just before going for the next treatment, eating became a pleasure once more, so I'd indulge in my favourite foods, tasting the purity of food again with every ingredient dancing on my taste buds and fireworks exploding in my mouth.

Chemo brain was another issue to deal with. A major one. The so-called pregnancy brain has nothing on this one. My memory was so muddled and foggy that on a daily basis I had to double check the simple things in life, like was I wearing underwear. Luckily, everyone around me understood, and the people I met during chemo were feeling the strain of memory loss too. It was a relief to talk to the other patients and laugh at ourselves—to know that what I was feeling was typical.

The whole routine was increasingly morphing into a newfound monotony. I learnt what to expect, when to expect it, what not to expect, what to take for it, find new changes in my body, accept them, what appointments I needed to get to, what I had to bring to them, and so on.

What I didn't expect was what I saw in the mirror. Scarified stripes were surfacing on my shoulders, my neck and my back. Initially, I wasn't too happy to see them, but staring at them in the mirror, they grew on me.

I discovered they are called chemo stripes and it's thought that the Bleomycin causes them. All I knew was that they were to become my battle scars. I fell in love with them back then and I'm still in love with them today for what they represent. My survival.

13

FIND WHAT MAKES YOU HAPPY

Treatments seven and eight

Menstrual cycles. As confronting as this may be, I'm going into this; for the women that may be feeling the same discomfort.

During this treatment cycle, I noticed an acrid odour coming from my period when changing my sanitary pad: a nasty, strong chlorine bleach-like smell that, as we all know, is not normal. I freaked out and kept it to myself for as long as I could, too embarrassed and ashamed to talk to anyone else.

Holding my breath didn't stop me from gagging. My femininity withered away even more after this started. The hospital list of side effects included irregular menstrual cycles, but the only irregular thing I experienced with my cycles was the chemical smell.

I also noticed that I could be outside at all hours of the night with not one single mosquito bite. That was definitely a chemo perk. Something to do with the smell in the blood stream, maybe?

I had to reclaim some of my femininity back, and my nails were a good way to start. I went to a nail salon to have a full set of acrylics applied, spoiling myself so at least a part of me could be beautiful, while the rest of me felt like a walking wreckage.

The exhaustion of chemo started during this time, peaking during the first week after treatment. Lying in bed or on the couch, I would try to move my arms and hands, but they felt like immovable lead weights.

Light exercise was recommended by my doctors for both my physical and psychological well-being, but all of my bones and joints had been replaced with cement. Getting up and moving to go for a walk took a tremendous amount of willpower.

Gaining weight from the steroids in my treatment, I followed their advice and went for a walk. I didn't enjoy one second of it. The overpowering fatigue intertwined with frustrating boredom, plus the onslaught of my thoughts following me the entire time—I would have preferred the sanctuary of my couch. What was the point of walking when my brain wouldn't switch off and I couldn't stop yawning?

It was three in the morning after treatment eight and I was beset by the usual onset of insomnia I normally had after treatment. I'd taken two strong Valium tablets to try and sleep. Through the heavy and hazy sedation of the Valium mixed with the jitteriness of the Dexamethosone, I watched the typical infomercials, bored out of my brain.

One in particular caught my attention: Zumba® fitness DVD ads showed people dancing around and jumping like crazy, laughing and having fun. Thinking how much I'd love to be a part of that, I ordered the DVDs. I had nothing to lose, and if nothing else I'd save them for when I was in remission and cancer clear.

Remission . . . a dream that was getting closer, or I hoped so, anyway.

After seeing the positive PET scan weeks earlier, I imagined that the cancer had probably just about disappeared, and it became difficult to stay motivated and continue treatments. I was far too impatient and, although I only had four treatments left, I was well and truly over it.

By the end of that first week after chemo I felt pretty damn good—so good that I stopped taking my herbs. I figured I didn't need them anymore.

That afternoon, without the herbs, I felt myself quickly deteriorate and the next day I woke up a confused mess. It happened so fast I had absolutely no idea what was happening. The nausea was coming on strong to the point of dry retching again. I had to take the Emend (anti-vomiting meds), which I hadn't needed since starting the herbs through most of my treatment. In fact, I would only need the Emend the day of treatment. Never after.

Laden with exhaustion, an outbreak of stinging mouth ulcers ruptured throughout my mouth, my gums, even on my tongue. My skin broke out. My self-esteem was non-existent.

The next day, something that I had only experienced after the very first treatment hit me like an erratic runaway train: hopelessness, deep sadness, and the veil of darkness all came back stronger, faster and more powerfully than before. Another dark day.

Unfortunately for Dr Louis Cali, my acupuncture appointment was for the same day as the darkness had taken over my mind and my emotions. As I walked into the clinic, I was holding back tears and the confusion of not understanding where they were coming from depressed me even more. I thought I was going insane and planned to book in to see Dr Raj, too. Maybe I needed some happy pills.

Dr Cali asked me how the herbs were going, and I mentioned that I'd stopped taking them as I felt great a few days before and didn't need them anymore. As I said it, I burst into tears, telling him I didn't understand why I was being so emotional.

I wailed that it had been several months since the very first lymphoma symptoms had appeared, and I was still going through shit and feeling worse. I was tired of doctors and blood tests and chemo and not being normal, living on a different planet of cancer and medications. I felt like an outcast, a loner, with no one understanding me and no one to talk to about it.

He listened to me the entire time like a psychiatrist. He suggested I continue the herbs, as my body needed the support, and basically told me to be nicer to myself. To be more sympathetic to the fact that I was a cancer patient and this was part and parcel of the treatment. I was going through a life-altering time and it was completely normal to lose hope.

The acupuncture was becoming unpleasant, too. I'd wince at every needle piercing the different parts of my body, upset that I couldn't enjoy acupuncture anymore. And I was angry that so many of the things I used to enjoy were changing fast.

I cried through the whole acupuncture treatment. I didn't want any of it anymore and wondered how different my life would be in that moment if this cancer hadn't been there

Although I felt better after seeing Dr Cali, the darkness still hounded me.

I went to see Dr Raj the day after taking no herbs, and asked for a prescription for a good dose of happy pills. Emotionally crazy, I broke down crying to him, too! Of course! What was wrong with me?

Dr Raj refused to give me anything. He sat back in his chair, smiling, crossed his arms over his chest and told me that it was absolutely normal to have emotional breakdowns, sort of scolding me as a father would his daughter. He believed in me more than I believed in myself.

He prescribed rest and acceptance instead. Well, that wasn't fair. I still wanted happy pills. I wanted an easier way out.

When I got home later that night, I broke down to Mum, too. Why not cry to everyone, Karina, I thought to myself, infuriated for being this weak, victimised person.

My mum, the wise woman she is, caught on straight away. She asked me if I had taken my herbs. I said no because I had been feeling great. Well, it doesn't matter how old I am, I still get reprimanded. And I finally understood what was happening. It had been a dark *three* days this time, more severe than the first episode, because the toxic build up had increased significantly by treatment eight compared to treatment one.

This was all the evidence I needed to firmly believe with all my heart that the herbs were supporting and helping my body, shielding me from dark days and protecting me from the harshness of chemo. It couldn't be a coincidence.

I started taking my herbs again that very night. By the next morning, the darkness began lifting slowly and a modicum of energy returned. By the afternoon, the nausea had eased and I was myself again, apart from the typical mild fatigue.

Treatments nine and ten

When treatment nine rolled around, the pinnacle of heavy fatigue mingled with the force of nausea soared. Utterly exhausted, the finish line was too distant—the light at the end of the tunnel was now dulled to an opaque, pin-sized dot.

My girlfriends were going out that same weekend and invited me along. Determined to break out of the fatigued rut I was in, I couldn't wait to get out of the house, to dress up and feel like a woman again.

By this time, the hair on the top of my head was extremely thin. Although I had managed to keep some of my hair, my scalp was clearly visible and light would reflect off it through the remaining strands of hair.

Embarrassed, I tried on different beanies and headscarves to hide it. I didn't feel attractive or sexy at all, but in the end I chose to wear my shiny scalp proudly. I was fighting cancer!

As soon as we walked into the club, I rushed to the dance floor. I felt myself smiling as I closed my eyes, feeling the bass line hitting the floor and snaking its way up through my feet. This was my world. This was what I loved. This was my normal. I wasn't Karina the cancer patient, or Karina the mum. I was just Karina, escaping all the bullshit I was going through out in the real world. I was allowed to forget in that moment everything to do with illness.

Through the night, my legs became so stiff and sore that I had to sit down. Going into the DJ booth, I sat against the wall and let the beat of the music thump through my head, pushing all of my thoughts aside and letting the music take me to another place. I closed my eyes and imagined myself never having cancer. I loved it.

I was in there for a good hour before the fatigue finally brought me back to reality and the desperation to go home became stronger than the need to be there. I was proud of myself for lasting as long as I had, and I'd discovered a new type of freedom: dancing and music.

Following treatment ten, it was time to shave my head for The World's Greatest Shave. With so many wonderful people around us during that time, we managed to raise over $3000 for the Leukaemia Foundation. I'd approached the primary school my daughters attend, and they arranged a crazy hair day for the foundation, raising well over $2000.

At the last minute, I admit I had second thoughts. Even though my hair had dramatically thinned out and my hairline was disappearing, I had managed to keep my hair. My eyebrows had vanished. My eyelashes were just stumps on my eyelids. But some of my hair had held on.

Apart from that, my scalp had adjusted to the burning and bruised sensations. Being so close to the finish line of treatment, I felt it was a shame to shave off my remaining hair. Nonetheless, I wanted to do it for The Leukaemia Foundation and for all the patients it helped and required funding for.

As it was the day after receiving my treatment, I felt awful, overwhelmed with nausea, but Tracy had organised a surprise shave party complete with helium balloons to match my voice (very funny), streamers and food. Everything was decorated in purple, representing Hodgkin's lymphoma. I was taken aback. My friends had gone to so much trouble that I was speechless. I didn't think it was that important, but they made me feel special, which brought more tears to my eyes.

Mel was dying to give me a mohawk, so I let her, only because Tracy was there ready with the clippers to save my hair and my reputation. With a vodka in my hand, the shaving began and the emotions and tears threatened to break through the strong mask I had fixed on my face.

I watched my hair falling to the floor, mourning its passing. As the last of my hair was swept away, I forced back the tears and chose to concentrate on the amount of money I had raised. It was worth every strand.

I had no chance to cry anyway, not with Mel or Tracy in the house. I had to suck it up and keep going, as they styled me with scarves, beanies and hats. It suddenly didn't seem so bad. I could have fun with this new look. When they ripped out the wigs, I morphed into Salt'n'Pepa, breaking into the running man dance. No, not a good look.

The party started with Mel sucking in the helium balloons, and breaking into a song. A rendition of *Black Velvet* that Alvin and the Chipmunks would be proud of.

Half way through my drink, my chest started to throb. I threw the drink down the sink, secretly trying to figure out why my chest was aching. Concluding that my body must be sensitive to the alcohol, I didn't give it another thought.

Treatments eleven and twelve

The last two treatments were the cruellest: a devastating brew of nausea, exhaustion and deliriousness, and exasperation with chemo and doctors and hospitals, bored with blood tests and scans and medications, and lost with no hair and no eyelashes and faded eyebrows and no self-esteem. While I was kicking cancer's arse, chemo was kicking mine.

I couldn't feel the tips of my fingers anymore. No matter how hard I pressed into them, they felt nerveless. I was eager to crawl over the finish line which was so near, yet so far at the same time. That was when I had to dig deep to find every last morsel, every last drop and fragment of strength I could find, and pull it all together to envision a happily ever after.

A few days after treatment eleven, I came home to my long-awaited Zumba® fitness DVDs. As if answering my prayers, they sat at the front door, waiting for me. I sat down to watch one of the discs on my laptop.

Latino beats sliced through the room. I looked around wondering where the music was coming from, when I realised it was coming from the DVD on the laptop. Immediately engrossed in the beats of the opening credits, I read the back of the cover and saw the words salsa, merengue and reggaeton.

What? For some reason, I had been oblivious to the fact that it was a Latin-based fitness program. It was so late at night when I had ordered them and the volume had been muted, that all I had seen was a group of people dancing around and laughing. All of a sudden, I wasn't so tired anymore.

The Latin fire in my veins started pulsing to the drums in the warm-up track, so I hooked up the speakers in Paul's studio and skipped ahead to the cumbia track. I swear I stopped breathing. Memories and flashbacks of my mother's beloved Colombia flooded my mind and my spirit, with the sounds of the accordion blaring in the studio.

Those were the years when I had given up modern dancing and developed a strong connection to Latin dancing instead. I'd unknowingly drift into the music, teaching myself the moves to the different dance styles we have, every day, until I naturally became a part of them. Because they already were a part of me.

I burst into tears—happy and proud tears that streamed down my cheeks as I called out for my parents to come and watch with me.

They'd heard the music too, and were already on the way to the room. I couldn't believe my ears. I couldn't believe my *eyes*. I was watching our culture on the screen. It was our dancing style that people were having fun with. It was our music that everyone was yelling to!

Finally, the Latino culture had made it in a good way. All through school I'd had to put up with taunts and bullying because of my culture. I'd get teased about growing cocaine in my backyard and being part of the Mafia. People were so narrow minded, only believing what they hear on the news, and assuming that drugs and violence was the only way of life for the Latino culture.

But here, right in front of me, danced a Colombian man, front and centre. I would soon find out his name was Beto, and he was dancing to the rhythm of our country, bringing something beautiful from our culture to the forefront, for people everywhere to witness who we really are.

I stood up and attempted to walk through the steps. I laughed at myself and felt like a total idiot, having to stop and catch my breath a few times because it was too intense and too fast. My father kept telling me to sit down and just watch, reminding me that I'd had treatment only a few days before. But I didn't care. I was happy! An emotion I hadn't felt the purity of for such a long stretch of time.

I promised myself I would find the will to walk through the steps everyday, to help my body become fit and healthy again; to help restore my lungs to how they were supposed to be; to get lost in that happiness, even if only for five minutes.

Reading something about becoming an instructor on the back of the pack, I watched one of the lead instructors on there, Gina Grant. She's a mother of four and one hell of a dancer. I watched her in awe as she motivated me through the screen to dance to her amazing level and feel her passion resonate with every move. I visualised myself strong and healthy and beautiful. In my entire life, I had never had an idol, until then. Gina became my inspiration.

And now, after stumbling across this new dance program, I had a new reason to keep going . . . to keep fighting.

After repeating the track twice, I realised that I had been smiling and laughing the entire time. Just when I thought I'd lost my smile, it was back, uninhibited and breaking through the tribulations of the past six months. It was then that I turned to my mum and said, 'You know what? There needs to be something like this, something fun but much easier. Something especially designed for people like me, for us cancer patients. We deserve it too.' And the concept for Liberation™ was born.

March 2010

At the last treatment, Tracy and another close girlfriend, Adele, decided to come with me to chemo. I knew I was in for an amusing day.

Before giving me any chemo, the nurse double-checked the blood test levels. She went back and forth, making sure she was holding the correct results form. Incredibly, my red blood cell count had been increasing throughout chemo, and not declining.

I had started on 125, and now I was at 138. It didn't make much sense to her, but I smiled. It wasn't due to a miracle or freak accident of nature. I knew deep down it was thanks to the herbal formulae and I couldn't wait to tell Dr Cali at our next appointment.

So, as the day dragged on, we were all on our best behaviour, but as children do when they get bored sitting in the same place hours on end, so do adults. Well, the adults I was surrounded by. With our group, it was destined.

Adele was trying to classify the perfect holiday destination while flipping through a magazine. Coming across an advertisement for a vacation package deal for Phi Phi Island, she announced, 'Oooh, Fi Fi Island sounds amazing,' to which Trace and I doubled over in a fit of laughter. The entertainment for the other patients had begun.

Adele was completely oblivious as to why we were laughing, which made it even more entertaining, as she is a highly educated woman. 'It's pronounced Pee Pee Island, Deli,' Tracy explained, through a failed attempt of a straight face. We had every other patient in the ward giggling under their breaths, while Adele fumed, mumbling to herself something about p'otograp'y, and autograp's,' as she flipped the pages of the magazine.

My family arrived later that afternoon to take the reins from my friends, and it was just as wonderful to spend that last hour of chemo surrounded by them. A surreal and unforgettable celebration. This was it. This was really it!

When the nurse disconnected my PICC line from the last saline bag, I hugged her and went around thanking all of the nurses for helping me, for being an incredibly huge part of my journey for the past six months. They had made every treatment day easier.

Walking out of that last treatment was a moment so monumental, it's very hard to put into words. A tremendous pressure lifted off my shoulders and I didn't care that I felt terrible. I was so elated that nothing could stand in my way. I did it! After everything, after riding the biggest emotionally and physically draining wave, I came out of it.

Pride and satisfaction that I had beaten cancer filled every part of me. I would never doubt myself or my body again.

My family were over the moon. We had all been in this battle together, and we had fought united until the end.

Totally exhilarated, I held my own closing ceremony at home. Tempted to pile every last box of medication and treatment booklets in my backyard and burn them in a bonfire, I opted to use the bin instead. I ripped all the booklets in half and threw every packet of medication and painkillers associated with chemo away. The library of resources I had collected relating to cancer went with them. Everything. I never wanted to see anything like them again.

I had made it.

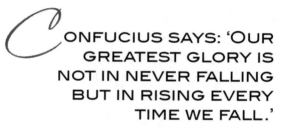

ONFUCIUS SAYS: 'OUR GREATEST GLORY IS NOT IN NEVER FALLING BUT IN RISING EVERY TIME WE FALL.'

Seeing the haematologist again would bring me crashing back down to Earth. As there was a slight chance I had lingering cancer cells lying dormant in my chest, I was encouraged to start radiation therapy to blast them away. If I didn't have radiation the following month, the possibility of the lymphoma returning increased. I had always known it was a possibility, but I was entirely unaware of the extent of my next path.

Having radiation meant that I was to go in to the hospital every day for three and a half weeks. Seventeen daily treatments. 'Oh, kill me now,' I thought. Just when I thought I was free, I was caught again in its web. Another crossroad.

I was booked in for the initial consultation where the technicians would explain the procedures of my new journey. As much as I was grateful for everything, I began resenting the hospital. My patience was wearing thin.

Obviously, there were more side effects and long-term effects associated with radiation therapy: secondary cancers, fatigue, lung damage, a decrease in lung function, breathing difficulties, hypothyroidism, heart disease, localised hair loss, itching or redness of the skin in the area being treated, nausea, mild burns, difficulty swallowing, dry mouth and irritation, change in taste. Easy. With what I'd just been through, this would be a piece of cake!

The radiation I was to have was called local therapy, and was done externally with a machine using high-energy rays to kill cancer cells. I had pin-sized tattoos done, which are used to line up the chest and neck area with the laser lights of the machine, and guide the technician to where to target the treatment. A quick and easy procedure.

I felt like a badass with my new tattoos.

I had to wait five weeks before I could start radiation, giving my body a break in between treatments. I decided to keep taking the herbal formulae while waiting, just in case.

Transitioning into this new chapter was difficult. I'd wake up in the morning, not needing to take any anti-nausea medication, and with no need to rush off to a blood test or doctor appointments. It felt so strange that I felt almost lost, as if I'd just stepped into a twilight zone.

April 2010

With most of the chemo symptoms gone, the only one that remained was relentless exhaustion. It happened that my birthday fell in the short break between treatments, and even though I didn't particularly feel like seeing anyone or partying, I felt like celebrating coming out of chemo, achieving remission, and living to see my birthday.

Tracy, Adele and Mel were adamant that I should do something to revel in the moment, but because I couldn't face too many people at that point, we chose to keep it small. Only Bec couldn't make it at the last minute. Outside of my family, my almighty support team was composed of these few strong women.

They had all been with me through the journey, with daily phone calls, text messages, voice mails, escape homes, or looking after my children and, they never gave up on me.

This was the first night in almost six months where I could be myself and really let my 2mm 'hair' down.

We started the night by having dinner at our favourite restaurant and partied the only way we knew how—with strawberry daiquiris and an abundance of Italian food. I was in heaven.

Even though I was concerned that I shouldn't be drinking so soon after chemo, a part of me didn't really care. I deserved it and I couldn't wipe the smile off my face.

The party continued at Tracy's house, with Mel, the only sober one (for once, and definitely not happy about it), as our chauffeur.

We laughed, talked, drank and lap danced one another until sunrise, on the back porch, not caring about the neighbours and the amount of noise we were making. It was one of the most liberating and healing nights I remember after chemo.

A few days later, I began reflecting back on everything I'd been through. The good with the bad. I went back through the archive of childhood memories that lay dormant in my subconscious: my past, saved onto a permanent hard drive in the back of my mind.

It was then that I noticed I'd had a small breakthrough. In that moment, most of the torment connected to my past had dissolved. It didn't matter anymore. Cancer had somehow helped me release it.

May 2010

The radiation treatments themselves were quite relaxing and easy, much like getting an X-ray, lying down to receive treatment while the machine circled around me. But going in daily became an exhausting feat near the end.

In this new adjustment my life revolved around radiation.

The day I stopped the inner whingeing about this was when I bumped into Amy, the beautiful woman I'd met in chemo. The inspiring lady with bowel cancer who had forced me to look at myself and admire my own journey. She was calling my name, only I didn't recognise her at first.

Amy was in a wheelchair, pale and gaunt, her eyes huge with dark circles under them. She had lost a tremendous amount of weight and her newfound baldness was hidden under a beanie. It wasn't so much the physical changes I didn't recognise—the inspirational light in her eyes and the contagious smile she had when I'd first met her had disappeared. Amy was dying.

She began explaining the last month of her personal hell to me. 'They won't tell me anything more than what I don't want to know. The only thing I do know is that the cancer was rejecting the chemo and is becoming more aggressive and growing faster by the day, so my doctor stopped my chemo treatments. There is nothing more they can do. I don't understand it, Karina. I don't understand why this happened, or why this is happening to me,' she broke into sobs, moaning into her tissue.

I grabbed her hand and cried with her, looking into her terrified eyes. She was so lost. The person I'd met in chemo wasn't there anymore.

I didn't know what to say. I hated hearing, 'Just be positive and be strong, you'll get through it,' when I was fighting to survive. How can you say that to someone losing their battle?

'They want to try radiation, just to try to slow the growth of the tumour and help me with the pain. They can't stop it from growing any more and the pain is absolutely excruciating. It's the only hope I have left. I know I don't have long, Karina.' She stopped to catch her breath and wipe her tears.

'They took my husband into a private room and told him more, but I don't want to know. I don't want to have a time limit.' I felt like I was in slow motion again. I looked from him to her in disbelief. I couldn't understand how this was happening. How could this beautiful woman sitting in front of me be dying? She had been so positive. So strong! But those incredible attributes hadn't worked? Why? How was I coming out of cancer, and she wasn't?

Her partner mouthed to me over her head as she cried into her tissue so she couldn't see, 'She doesn't have long. Maybe a month.' He sadly smiled at me with sincerity and deep sorrow in his eyes. He had been hiding his affliction behind his smile, and I thought of Paul then, because that's how Paul would look at me.

A part of me died inside. This is cancer in all its fucking glory. I'd been blindfolded in denial, choosing not to acknowledge the torment it can be for other patients, choosing not to see death as the final result, for my own sanity and survival.

And while I'd been complaining about having radiation every day, this is what others have to face, forced to say goodbye to a life they don't want to let go of. Their loved ones are left behind to pick up the pieces and live with the emptiness left in their place.

But I was clear. My tumour was gone. My life was mine again.

Guilt weighed heavily on me. I was making it out of this, and Amy along with many others wouldn't get that chance.

I cried through my treatment and all the way home. I wished I'd taken the time to write Amy's number down and keep in touch with her. Her story affected me for days afterwards, her memory forever embedded with me.

My perspective changed again. From that moment, I chose to be grateful for my journey, to show myself, and my life, appreciation. To be thankful to be alive.

Before treatments I would go for a walk in the surrounding streets, slowly building my fitness level from fifteen-minute walks to forty-five-minute walks. I had been so used to hiding out in my house that it felt good to get out and exercise.

I visualised myself cancer-free and healthy while taking in the deep breaths I had craved only months before. I loved the feeling of fresh air in my lungs. It was my tonic before radiation, before the nauseating hospital smells would invade my senses. I visualised myself on stage, dancing freely without a care in the world, talking myself through affirmations that I would be there soon, believing them as I spoke.

After every radiation treatment, I would send prayers of love and strength to Amy and her family. She continued living in my thoughts. Amy had shown me the light by the magnetism in her smile, the strength in her determination and the wonder of life in her eyes, and I give thanks to her for sharing that piece of her life with me. In my heart, she was an incredible survivor.

Amy, thank you.

June 2010

Upon finishing radiation, a mixture of relief, confusion and sadness permeated the air. Everything to do with cancer and treatments had become such a colossal part of my life that I felt safer while going in to treatments. As excited as I was to finish them, I walked out of the last treatment thinking, 'So now what?' I was left to fend for myself.

I had some side effects from the radiation, starting with a sore throat—every time I swallowed, I felt like a ball with spikes was attaching itself to the back of my tongue. I had become increasingly fatigued and developed a rectangular patch of red radiation burn on my chest like sunburn, which eventually peeled and then tanned to a darker patch.

In the hospital, they discussed the importance of looking after your body through nutrition and sun care, with no sunbathing for three years. They recommending applying SPF 30+ sun protection when outside. But for whatever reason, it didn't apply to me.

As much as I tried, it was difficult to pick up my life where I had left off pre cancer. Pre cancer normality no longer existed for me. That was a world where I'd had no ailments, no symptoms, no cancer.

For almost a year, my life revolved around cancer, and during that time my life had been put on hold, while the world continued spinning around me. How do you go back to life before cancer when so much of your life has changed? How was I supposed to go back to being me? Who was I?

Fighting cancer was all I knew. It was part of me, my identity. I wasn't sure how to close that chapter. With cancer gone, I had to find a new normal, slamming on the brakes to change gears from fighter to survivor, because in my mind the two were separate. It was only later when I came to realise that while I was fighting to survive, I was already surviving; living daily through the chaos of cancer.

Two weeks later at the last haematology appointment I had upon finishing radiation, the doctor told me to simply enjoy life. When I asked him if I should be wary of any foods or if I should avoid alcohol, he just told me to enjoy my life as much as I could, with everything in moderation. So that's what I did. Sort of. Without hearing the word 'moderation.'

The taste of freedom was sweet. Walking through the rain to my car, I stopped suddenly on the path and looked up, closing my eyes, feeling the coolness of the rain drops falling on my face. I smiled as I watched everyone around me scramble to their cars in a hurry. I was free. I was finally free.

In the balancing act of life, I threw myself into the opposite end of the scale from illness. I went to extremes, drinking alcohol until I was inebriated and eating copious amounts of junk food and sugary sweets, savouring every mouthful. I was immortal and untouchable and life is too short. I'm a survivor, right? I could survive anything.

As far as I was concerned, I would never get cancer again and I didn't have to worry about food or herbs. I didn't have to worry about anything!

So desperate for a sliver of normality, I did everything in my power to have fun.

Going to the cinemas with Adele to watch the premier of *Sex and the City* was an adventure and a half.

I brought bottles of vodka and lemonade with me. Eyeing my beverages, Adele asked me, 'Are you sure you want to do this my girl?'

'Yes!' I screamed, 'I *need* this!'

I couldn't have had a more perfect person to share the evening with. We walked into the cinema armed with plastic champagne flutes, walking in a straight line, completely sober and excited to celebrate this monumental event.

When we walked out, we were bumping into walls, laughing hysterically.

The night didn't end there. We fashionably sloshed our way into a restaurant and tried most of the cocktails on the menu. The more people would look at me and my shaved head with harsh judgement and criticism (or so I thought), the more I would drink, to prove to everyone, including myself, that I was normal.

Even though we'd had a wonderful night, I was privately depressed, overweight, confused and lost. My life wasn't bouncing back into the carbon copy of who I was before cancer.

In a bizarre twist, a part of me missed the appointments I was used to and the sense of having something to fall back on. Remission was something I had looked forward too for so long that I couldn't understand the emptiness I felt once I'd reached it.

Urgently wanting to find myself again, I immersed myself into Zumba® fitness. Dancing was the only normal thing I knew, and it was like reclaiming an essential part of me that had vanished many years ago. I trained hard everyday with the DVDs, pushing my body to the limit for the entire hour, sometimes more, and I loved it. Regardless of having to stop to catch my breath every few minutes, the smile I'd find was exhilarating.

It was the only hour or so where I could laugh and be completely stupid with Jaivan as my only audience. On the days I was too tired, Jaivan would be the one to hand me the DVD and tell me to dance. He loved watching and would dance with me. My partner in crime. We had so much fun together, bashing into each other while he'd step all over my feet.

My family would become concerned, telling me to slow down and take it easy. My mum said to me, 'Karina, you just came out of chemo. Take it easy girl!'

Subconsciously, I jammed my fingers in my ears—I didn't want to hear it. I was fine. I kicked cancer's arse. I could do anything!

I joined Zumba® classes with no self-confidence and overweight. I'd refuse to look in the mirrors because I hated what I saw. I didn't recognise my own reflection: a mere stranger looking back at me, following my every move and expression. Short hair, swollen and pudgy, ugly with dark circles under her eyes.

I'd close my eyes and lose myself in the music and the movements, escaping my reality. I wasn't a mum. I wasn't a cancer patient. I was me. And for the first time in a long time, I was unrestricted, not having to follow any rules or procedures. I was happy, even if it would only last for a brief amount of time.

Ignoring what my body needed after treatment, I didn't look after myself. I threw myself into daily fitness training. Walking, dancing in the kitchen, anything I could do to keep going. As far as I was concerned, I'd never had cancer.

October 2010

Four months into remission, I had lost a tremendous amount of weight—twenty-two kilograms to be exact—and I found a renewed zest for life. I became a Zumba® instructor and began holding my own classes. Ironically, the day I became an instructor fell on my 'cancerversary': one year to the day since I'd had my first chemo treatment. I took it as a sign of closing one door and opening another.

Getting my certification was life-changing, an exceptionally emotional moment. I'd worked so hard *for* my life through chemo and radiation, that I deserved this as a reward. Exactly one year and two months of working my backside off for a glimpse of health, happiness and freedom.

Everything I'd fought for came down to this very moment. It had been thirteen years since I'd quit dancing, and I never thought I'd be able to dance again, but I'd done it. A lifelong dream was materialising.

I ignored the smell of chemicals radiating from my body in the training sessions, and in every class I instructed from then on. I didn't want to know. The smell would seep into my clothes during and after training. I knew the chemo drugs were being cleansed out of my body through my pores. I just hoped no one around me could smell it.

My trainer, Maria Teresa Stone, was another person on my list of inspirational people, besides Gina Grant, within the program. She had so much energy and passion that she was an absolute dream to watch, and an explosive instructor.

I love my job, helping people reach their goals and a happiness that I know all too well about, through music and dance. Even during a bad day, one class can turn it around.

But while I was busy helping everyone else through the fourteen weekly classes of rigorous fitness and exercise, I was denying myself any chance of healing. I was starving my body of essential nutrition and bombarding it instead with excessive amounts of exercise, sunbathing to a crisp, alcohol and junk food. Everything I'd learnt about my health and body went out the window.

Sadly, when I was home, I didn't want to be there, because home was a reminder of cancer. Home had been my hibernating place for so long that all I wanted was to be free and dance.

What I didn't realise at the time was that not only was I hurting myself, I was hurting my family. They had been through the journey with me and had been hurting just as much as I had. They needed to heal just as much as me.

Healing for them meant being around me, and sharing in my life. Broken hearted from missing her mum, my daughter Aaliyah had cried to her *abuela*, 'Where's Mama? Doesn't she love us anymore'?

Dancing had always been my way out of emotional pain and traumas throughout my childhood. I was always so busy with rehearsals and performing on stage that it didn't give me any time to look at anything else, and I loved it. And now, I was unknowingly doing it again, throwing myself into classes and rehearsing daily, so soon after having cancer.

In the throes of denial, I was strongly avoiding the process of accepting the journey I had just been on, and I had no idea how to snap out of it. So I kept going, running on pure adrenalin. The more classes the better. The less I had to look at myself, my cancer and the past year, the happier I was. I was not a cancer patient anymore. I was me, and nothing was going to take this happiness and exhilaration away from me.

15

FINDING A BALANCE

January 2011

My body had started struggling with the unhealthy imbalance I was entangled in. The onset of fatigue and weakness began taking a toll on me, and had started weeks earlier, but I'd stubbornly refused to acknowledge it. I was hitting a wall. With a poor diet and excessive amounts of exercise, not to mention blinkering myself from the last year and a half, it was no wonder.

The moment I had been hiding from was unavoidable and arrived sooner than I would have liked. I was to have my first routine PET scan since completing radiation therapy. This was a day when being a cancer patient was thrown back in my face.

I cried the whole way to the MRI, terrified that it was back. The fear that I had crushed for so long was now triggered. My gut instinct was screaming at me that something was going to come up. I had a feeling that all the neglect I had been hurling at my body was about to catch up with me.

I cried throughout the scan, with the memories of treatment and its side effects flooding back in flashbacks and the panic sickened my stomach.

A few days after the scan, Paul and I were sitting on our bed with our kids, blissfully happy to finally be spending some quality time with my family watching a movie, when the phone rang.

It was a doctor I didn't know.

He requested I book in with my regular GP for an appointment.

Why?

I begged him to tell me over the phone, because the suspense was killing me. Anxious and nervous, my mouth dried up into a familiar paste before he replied. I knew it was bad. He was trying to find the best way to tell me.

Hesitantly, he began explaining that the area in my chest where the tumour had been had traces of cells that had been lit up by the contrast material of the PET scan. The results had come back with a positive result of early stages of lymphoma.

No!

Despair and shock pulled at my heart as I thanked him quickly through tears in my eyes. I told him I'd book in with Dr Raj later that day, and hung up abruptly.

Dropping to my knees, I fell apart and sank back into the quicksand of emotions that were all too familiar to me. 'No . . . . not again! I don't want to go through it again! Please God. No!'

My survivorship was slipping through my fingers.

Paul grabbed me from behind and held onto me tightly and cried with me, burying his face into the back of my neck. He already knew. I didn't need to say anything.

I knew I shouldn't have been crying like this in front of my kids, but I couldn't hide it. I couldn't control it. I heard Paul quietly explain it to my kids while still holding onto me.

Aaliyah ran to me and slid into my arms, crying with us. 'No, Mama, not again. *Please.* I don't want you to do it again. I'm scared.' She looked up at me, tears falling down her beautiful face, while Monique looked on, confused. She was so little she couldn't understand what was happening.

My dad reached out to hold me as I fell into his arms and cried on his shoulder. The whole family fell apart with me. We were all in shock. Just when we had thought the crisis was over and we would never have to live through that again, it was back.

I couldn't concentrate on anything with all the questions circling around in my head. The worst part was that my eyes were wide opened and fully aware of what I was walking into. I'd already been there and done that.

Dr Raj was as shocked and deflated as I was, shaking his head in disbelief. Nonetheless, he remained positive, holding onto the possibility that it might not be cancer, that the lit up cells might not mean anything. It could also be due to swelling or inflammation in the area, which can be normal following treatment. But it didn't help the tug of war in my head.

Dr Raj gave me the results, knowing that this time around I would understand the report.

As I scanned through the findings, I came to a part where it stated, 'Given these findings, it raises the possibility of very early recurrence of mediastinal lymphoma.'

That sentence burned into my eyes.

What if it was more aggressive this time around? Doesn't that mean the treatment becomes more intense? What if I didn't make it out this time?

When I left his office and collapsed into my car, my world came crashing down. I held the steering wheel and cried until I couldn't breathe. How was I going to go through it all again? Why was this happening?

I phoned a naturopath I know, Sharon. She was a cancer survivor who had beaten the odds. She had gone through three horrendous battles with breast cancer and with her gruelling chemo regime, she had developed a pancreatic lesion.

The diagnosis was grim and the doctors suggested an even stronger chemo regime with radiation. Sharon took control, and with her extensive knowledge about nutrition, supplements and herbal remedies, resolved to do everything she could to help her body return to homeostasis. Five weeks later at another scan, she was in remission. She was my inspiration that I too could help my body through this.

Upon examining my blood through a live blood analysis (microscopic analysis of living blood cells), Sharon observed the physical changes expected due to the chemo in my blood cells.

Sharon then began educating me on the importance of nutrition. Cancer is known to grow in acidic environments influenced by the foods we eat and other determining factors such as stress, smoking and lack of sleep. We can help counteract cancer, so to speak, through changing our diet by increasing alkalising foods, therefore balancing the body into a more alkalised state.

It seemed too good to be true, and if Sharon weren't sitting in front of me, in full remission, healthy and happy, I wouldn't have believed it myself. Her story is incredible.

At home, I phoned Dr Cali. I wanted to resume the Chinese herbal formulae and he agreed straight away, as some of the herbs in the mix were also proven to neutralise cancer cells. Dr Cali also mentioned the influence of nutrition and cancer cells, and how alkalising the PH levels in the body may help hinder the development of cancer cells.

I began researching all of these things for myself, because I'd learnt from my first journey that knowledge equalled inner power. I rummaged through the internet, purchased books, read up on every notion and opinion out there.

The first alkaline book I picked up was filled with amazing recipes and confirmed the information Dr Cali and Sharon had given me.

I read that acidity is increasingly common in Western society, especially over the last several decades. Most people experiencing health problems and chronic diseases such as cancer are overly acidic. The main influence on acidity and alkalinity is our diet. Apparently, within the typical Western diet there is an ongoing acidifying effect in the body due to the processed and fast food foods we consume.

Acid forms in the body when consuming most meats, processed carbohydrates (white pasta, white rice, etc.), dairy products, caffeine, sugar, alcohol and white flour.

Acidity can also be produced through physical and psychological stress, lack of sleep, and an imbalance caused by too much strenuous activity with not enough rest. That was what I had been doing. Fourteen classes a week with no rest. Was I digging my own grave?

An alkaline-forming diet is rich in green vegetables, including some raw foods, juices containing raw, fresh vegetables, fruits, and healthy oils.

Everything I'd been doing up until that point was a recipe for disaster: too much strenuous activity, not enough rest, and eating every acid-producing food under the sun. I had to do something about my diet and my lifestyle.

These books were essential, like my nutritional bibles. They had charts on alkaline-forming and acid-forming foods that were easy to follow and that would guide the reader to improved health and wellness.

With my alkaline list in hand, I went grocery shopping and filled my kitchen with all types of organic foods. Green leafy vegetables, strawberries, blueberries, free range and hormone free chicken (to eat in moderation), salmon, trout, flaxseed oil, virgin olive oil, avocados, lemons, oranges, pears, raw beetroot and broccoli for juicing, carrots, cucumbers, garlic, dark green leafy lettuce, spirulina, lentils, dandelion root tea, green tea, almond milk, basmati rice, quinoa cereals, rolled oats, fresh cinnamon and coconut oil.

I cut out bread, pasta, rice, fast food, chocolate, ice cream, pastries, alcohol, coffee, sodas, sugar, and everything else considered acid forming.

It was expensive and hard to adjust, but I preferred this new way of eating and looking after my body on the inside to having myself pumped with poison again. And even if I did have to go through chemo, I would keep following this diet and taking the Chinese herbal formulae. I had nothing to lose, only a healthy life to gain.

At the haematologist's, I saw the PET scan image showing the evil cells in my chest lit up like cancer cells, with an added area in the lymph nodes under my left arm. That was a new area. That's when I panicked.

The haematologist explained the same things that Dr Raj had explained; that sometimes the cells light up due to swelling or inflammation and that it didn't necessarily mean they were cancer cells.

When he mentioned inflammation, I recalled what Dr Cali had said about highly processed foods creating inflammation in the body.

In case it was cancer, I was placed on a 'watch and wait' for the following four months to wait for a tumour to grow (if one would), to take a sample from in a biopsy, just like my first journey.

What I could be facing in the event of a tumour forming was a stem cell transplant, or bone marrow transplant. This is where healthy stem cells are extracted before higher doses of chemotherapy are received, wiping all cells from the body. The stem cells are then returned to the patient, with a recovery time of one or two weeks in hospital, depending on the body's reaction.

He mentioned that six weeks is the required period to rest after a transplant. No classes. No strenuous activity. I would be put on a harsher chemo regime for four months with the possibility of radiation again.

As this new information began to sink in, I felt sick. All I could do was smile and nod, while I looked at the dark spots on the PET scan.

The stem cell transplant was the worst part of this recurring nightmare. Six weeks to full recovery? What about my kids? What about my life?

Faced with another biopsy, surgery, harsher chemo, radiation, more doctors and hospitals, and more blood tests, my head ached. Just when I thought I was free, I was being chained down again with an added stem cell transplant thrown into the chaos.

It was time I changed my path of self-destruction. I became adamant to use this 'watch and wait' time to prove to myself that a change of diet and lifestyle could alter the tumultuous regime I was headed into.

That same day, I went to have a needle biopsy under my left arm in the lymph node where the possible cancer cells had been detected. Using an ultra sound machine this time, it wasn't as daunting as the needle biopsy I'd had in my chest. While painful, it was a much easier procedure that was over in a matter of minutes.

With so many lymph nodes in that area, it was too difficult to be sure of which one needed a sample taken from. The technician had said there were a couple of swollen nodes, so he used those.

We were all acting on guesses and whims, but that's what forced me to look at the whole journey and replay memories of chemo and hospitals. Wanting nothing more than the next PET scans to come back completely cancer free, I had four months to try anything and everything.

I tried the detox foot spa that Sharon had given me. She had mentioned that it works by drawing toxins out of the body through the soles of our feet. If nothing else, it was an excuse to sit and rest.

I was surprised at the results. The water started out clear, but by the end of the session time, my feet were soaking in a putrid muck of black tar. It was gross. Seeing the change in water, I kept up this treatment twice a week, and eventually the water became clearer.

March 2011

When the needle biopsy results came back negative, there was undeniable relief, but it wasn't enough.

I dropped my classes back to two a week and dedicated myself to being a mum, wife and daughter. I took time out to rest my body. I stopped hiding behind my classes and decided to concentrate on my family. This was happening for a reason—there was no doubt in my mind.

I began working on the concept I'd thought of during chemo: Liberation™.

My vision was to do something for patients going through chemo and remission, using music and dance movements as a way to forget for a small period of time what they are going through, and break the monotony of treatments.

Encompassing my passion for dance and how much it has changed my life over the years, helping me find myself time and time again, I knew that the gentle and slower movements through Liberation™ could work. I would play the commercial music we hear on the radio every day, so people could relate to the songs, understand the lyrics and sing along to the words if they wanted to. Liberation™ would be about offering a gentle escape. A chance to feel normal again—to feel alive again.

I began researching dance and movement with cancer patients and I found many articles asserting the benefits of dance for patients with chronic illnesses and depression.

The American Cancer Society suggests that therapy through dance may improve a patient's mental and physical well being, and that gentle dance may be effective in relieving stress and improving self-esteem.

Patients' perceptions of their bodies improve, along with reduced stress, anxiety, and depression and a decrease in isolation, chronic pain, and body tension. Increased communication skills and feelings of well being improve a patient's quality of life.

Using my own experiences with cancer, I knew how physical changes and transformations could be difficult to accept throughout illness and treatment. With weight gain, hair loss, fatigue, post surgery scarring, and feeling lost and unrecognisable, a blow to self-esteem in most cases is inevitable, as it was with me.

I craved fun, and dancing and music had been my salvation, especially through the process of the last weeks of chemo and radiation. I wanted to bring that sexy back to others fighting and surviving their cancer.

My second possible diagnosis changed my perspective yet again. I was a cancer patient for a second time around. While the disease was not medically confirmed yet, emotionally and psychologically the cancer patient inside me had returned. I became serious about my life once more.

Knowing the positive reaction I'd had taking the traditional Chinese medicine during my first battle, I continued the fight on my own. Armed with my herbs, alkalizing nutrition, dancing and resting, and visualising myself healthy and happy every day, I was positive I couldn't go wrong.

With a determined smile and a newfound gratitude for this second chance, there was no way I could revisit chemo. Not again.

16

REBUILDING YOUR LIFE WHEN YOU HIT ROCK BOTTOM

April 2011

My mother had wanted to go on holiday for some time. With the stresses of looking after me and my family, they needed time out from cancer too.

Talking about their holiday dream destination, I became anxious as memories of earlier traumas from my adolescent years began resurfacing.

Why the hell was I thinking of that all of a sudden?

No, Karina. It's in the past. It's not important anymore. Forget it.

Shutting the chilling scenes down in my mind, I told myself to get over it and continued on my mission of helping my body hinder a possible tumour from developing through my new diet and Chinese herbal remedies. That had to be my focus.

Mild recurring pelvic cramps and aches began toward the end of the month, but I didn't think too much of them, connecting them as possibly a delayed chemo side effect causing irregularities in my cycle.

May 2011

The mild aches became stronger than the usual cramping that would naturally occur in a menstrual cycle, lasting through most of the month. That was odd.

I'd have to stop what I was doing in the mornings and breathe through the pain before I could keep going.

This definitely was not normal for me. I've never been one to have ongoing period pain, or aches. The other unusual symptom I'd noticed was that the cramping would envelope around my lower back and shoot down my legs.

Now what!

There was a possibility that I had developed endometriosis or adenomyosis since treatment but the ultrasound scan results came back clear and normal, so I was put on the contraceptive pill.

My research on both conditions described the symptoms exactly as what I had been feeling, however there was one nagging difference. I had no pains during the week of bleeding and my cycles were lighter, not heavier. The pains were mainly present in the three weeks between.

I thought again that it had to be something connected with chemotherapy. The awful chlorine odour that occurred through my menstrual cycles while undergoing treatment must have something to do with this, right?

To further investigate the pelvic pains, I was placed on a waiting list for a laparoscopy and hysteroscopy. Three to five years was the wait time for those tests.

June 2011

I became proficient at ignoring the pains. I had pretty much graduated from the art of living with pain and pretending it didn't exist, because I was fine and I had a tumour (maybe) to stop from growing. That was my ultimate mission.

Eventually the 'watch and wait' time was at an end, and it was time to go in for the PET scan that would determine whether I'd be traveling down the chemo and stem cell transplant road.

I was surprisingly calm through the scan, falling asleep while waiting for the radioactive material to spread through my body. I had done as much as I could to care for my body, behaving myself with the herbal formulae, while feeding my body with essential nutrition and vital foods to alkalise my system. My conscience was clear.

One week later, the results came back clear! No cells were lit up. That scan image was the best I'd seen in a long time and I was ecstatic. I don't know if what I had done changed anything, but at least I had tried and I hadn't given up. I had been proactive from the beginning and chosen to do something positive instead of victimising myself.

A few weeks later, I stood in my kitchen and looked out the window, asking myself why I had to go through all of that the second time around? What did I need to learn from it? And it hit me like a ton of bricks. *Life*. I needed to learn about life!

For most of my life, I thought I was happy, but I had never fully appreciated the beauty of life. I started crying, realising that this was a second chance to prove to myself that I could find the true meaning of *my* life.

Outside I saw everything through different eyes. The trees, the grass, the flowers. Everything I saw looked different, gleaming with brilliance, illuminating the purity and density of each colour. Everything was so brightly lit up that my eyes struggled to adjust to the light.

I walked over to the grass and felt the earthy sensation under my feet, inhaling the smell of nature blowing in the gentle breeze. It was magnificent and different.

Filling my lungs with a new taste of oxygen I'd never tasted before, and seeing this new interpretation of life, I closed my eyes and allowed myself to feel, taste, smell, and listen.

The breeze rustling through the leaves of the trees in our garden; the sounds of birds flying past, hearing the brush of sound their wings made through the air; savouring the new flavour of oxygen on my tongue. I'd never experienced anything like that before.

Every one of my senses was alert and I was so thankful to be alive. This was the world outside! I'd been swimming inside my own mind for so long, that it was nice to join in what I'd been missing for so long! With all this newness, I started laughing.

Tears of joy and pride streamed down my face—tears of finally understanding life with a profound yearning to be a part of it. And from crying I started laughing again until both morphed into one.

My chest expanded with love for life and for my body and my self. Anyone watching me would have booked me in to the next available psychiatrist, or asylum, but I didn't care. I no longer cared what anyone thought or said about me. I knew what I was feeling, and that's all that mattered. From that moment onwards I swore to live every minute, of every hour, of every day, appreciating all that life had given me and all I was about to receive. I would never again doubt my life or my path, because there is a much bigger picture, beyond anything I could see or comprehend, and I was just happy to be a part of it.

I made positive changes by avoiding people and situations that would only bring problems and hurt into my life, only wanting to be surrounded by people who enjoyed life. I didn't have time for drama or negativity. No more.

It was no longer my business what anyone thought of me. I may have come across as ignorant, but only

I know my truth and the extent of what I have been through. I became so protective over my newfound happiness and joy that I was determined it was not going to be taken away from me. Never again. I was taking back control of me.

August 2011

We reached a decision as a family to sell our house and separate from my parents. Not for anything bad, because nothing actually happened. What had needed to be done with my illness had been done, and we all needed to close that door to build a new one.

We all waved goodbye when driving away from our old house that had been our sanctuary for so long and held so many memories, both painful and sweet. From Jaivan's birth, to my father having a stroke, my mother losing all sense of taste and smell to a viral flu, and finally, my disease.

Arriving to our new home was like a breath of fresh air. A new chapter. A new beginning. Almost like the closure we all needed for a new life.

September 2011

Three months later, the contraceptive pill wasn't having any effect on my pelvic pain. If anything, the pains were worsening, so I stopped taking it. Paracetamol was no longer working and codeine became my new friend.

It was the only thing that would bring relief. Adjusting to life with this pain was demanding, as I was still instructing classes and being a mum. I began cancelling events. No more parties, no dinners. I closed myself off in my house. I couldn't stand it anymore.

Most of the time it felt as though I was giving birth to my uterus. The pain was like the last moments of contractions before the baby appears, when everything is tearing and ripping open with a burning pain and an ongoing progression, leaving me breathless and desperate for relief.

The alkalising diet became incredibly difficult to follow, and I'd find myself craving sugar, chocolate, enormous amounts of junk food. Comfort food.

November 2011

The uterine pains became impossible to live with but conventional medicine didn't offer any solutions.

I contacted a good friend of mine, Jodie, who has an extensive background in nutrition and believes wholeheartedly that nutrition plays a major role in our physical wellbeing.

Jodie advised me on foods that could help with my particular pains, associating them with a possible hormone imbalance. She knew of my history of cancer and treatment, and suggested not only greens and fresh foods, but also to include as many red foods in my meals and snacks.

Jodie explains her approach:

> In Karina's case, foods beneficial for her immune system and hormone rebalancing were advised and discussed. Foods such as proteins, live yoghurt, limited meat products due to the effect on the digestive system, green tea which contains a powerful antioxidant found to inhibit the growth of cancer cells and helps with immune function.
>
> I advised her to add red and purple foods to her diet, which are also rich in antioxidants and anthocyanins (which are known to help reduce inflammation). Examples such as beets were strongly suggested, which are also high in folate needed for growth and repair of new cells. The deep colour comes from betanin, a phytochemical that's thought to boost immunity. Fruits and vegetables such as blueberries, strawberries, red plums and tomatoes are also very beneficial with Vitamin C. Nuts, predominantly almonds, seeds, green vegetables, parsley, essential fats found in avocado and omegas are all good options for promoting good nutrition.
>
> Whole foods, natural consisting products, i.e. proteins, carbohydrates, fats, minerals, vitamins and water all help to support insulin metabolism and therefore support over all hormone balance. Processed foods and

sugar can result in an imbalance within the body as we respond very quickly to what is consumed. The body is very sensitive to what we eat so it is important that nutrient dense foods are implemented.

Following Jodie's advice, the pain would slowly subside to a dull ache on certain days and become easier to manage, but there were also days that the intensity of the cramps would increase again.

Two weeks into the plan, I woke up to intense cramping. Doubled over and screaming through the contractions and the explosions of pain that had me crippled on the bed, I couldn't move at all. The pain would shoot down my inner thighs and my legs, causing my heart to thump and race through an ache in my head. I'd breathe through the pain, screaming with every exhale.

In between the contractions, I'd be trembling and left soaking wet from writhing in pain. Why was pain hitting me again? Wasn't it enough to have it through cancer?

I phoned another good friend of mine, Maria Kafaltis, who is also a qualified holistic and transpersonal counsellor. I'd seen her many times in the past, because besides being a very good friend to me, she would morph into counsellor mode when I needed her. I didn't know what else to do, and enough was enough.

Maria suggested that holistic counselling sessions might discover the cause of the pain. She explained that past emotional trauma often has a connection to our physical body, and illnesses or ailments can develop due to suppressing or repressing emotional pain. Sounded too technical for me, especially with the pain I was in, but it was time to admit that I needed help.

Maria explains:

> In Karina's case, I felt that the integrative nature of the physical, emotional, mental and spiritual aspects through holistic counselling techniques would be beneficial and would be able to provide a balance which would assist in the healing of her emotional, mental and spiritual state.
>
> Trauma generally takes anywhere from months to years to heal fully, if at all. Karina's case is an exception. Having battled a life-threatening illness, Karina was empowered by a renewed sense of what it means to be alive. Her new-found appreciation for life motivated her to work with and heal any past traumas, with an awareness and conviction that is not only rare, but inspiring.

During our first session a parade of haunting memories played through my head. It seems I wasn't over these past injuries, and I couldn't understand why these thoughts were bombarding me again.

I cried to Maria and told her everything I was feeling. She suggested we use a technique called focussing. Since Maria was well aware of my aversion to counselling, the holistic way seemed less threatening to me. Maria explained that through the focussing session, it was possible I would gain a deeper understanding of the physical pain by speaking with it.

Excuse me? Was she kidding? If I hadn't trusted Maria, and if she hadn't been one of my good friends, I would have thought she was nuts. If I wasn't so lost, I would have probably gone with, 'thanks, but no thanks,' and walked out on her.

What normal person talks to pain? Or, better yet, *how* does one talk to pain? I was desperate for help and I trusted Maria would only do what she felt was right for me. So, reluctantly, I agreed.

Pangs of contractions would pause the session for a couple of minutes until I was able to get my breath back. Maria started with breathing exercises to calm me down and help me focus on what we were about to do and guide me through the process.

Through the session, there were so many emotions coming out of it, that Maria asked if I would be comfortable drawing them to express what I was feeling. Art therapy.

Well, I can't draw. How the hell do you draw emotions? But, somehow, once the pencils were in my hand, there was no stopping me. My unartistic flurry of stick figures expressed what I had seen. When I was finished, I stopped to look at the picture in front of me, and it took my breath away.

On the table was a picture of a broken and scared stick figure with arms and legs broken off in pieces, surrounded by a dark red crayon scribbled haze. Picasso would roll in his grave. But it surprised me because I had no idea I could do that, that I had the capacity to see something like that, let alone draw it. I began crying again, as the shock of the lucid truth was right there on paper. There was no denying what was happening in my subconscious.

I felt a renewed satisfaction, because the session helped me put the pieces back together. Being bashed and molested on two separate occasions in my youth had morphed into one event in my subconscious. My memories of being broken and scared and feeling like a failure were part of a continuous loop that I had been living for so many years, denying myself the relief of letting go.

Now it was time to heal it, to deal with it properly.

Maria asked me what I wanted to do with the drawing, and I had a huge desire to tear it up, rip it to shreds, like a closure. I wanted to let that part of myself go, so I did, and it felt incredible.

After our first session, I was astounded and proud of myself. I'd never done any form of meditation before and it helped that Maria guided the entire process. I'd tried on my own but never got anywhere. Silence the mind, silence the mind. How do I silence something so uncontrollably talkative that never seems to shut up? My mind has a mind of it's own.

The way Maria guided that process was amazing, and I looked forward to being pain free soon.

Unfortunately, the next day, the pain was there again, in full force. It was getting harder to follow Jodie's nutritional advice, but I tried.

I waited a week before going to see Maria again, disheartened. I was hoping the session would get rid of the pain, but I needed to be patient, just like the waiting game before chemo and radiation all over again.

I didn't feel like doing any more of those processes. I wasn't ready. I just wanted to talk. The previous session was so full on and I wasn't sure if I believed that this holistic stuff would work, and I was impatient because the pain was still tearing through my insides. So, we talked about my experiences and any changes I had felt during the week between sessions. I needed to collect all the fragments and make meaning of the experience.

The enormous emotional relief of that first session was incredibly healing. Letting go of those last remnants of pain derived from those memories was a huge release. Maria helped me to not only forgive the emotions of the traumas themselves, but she guided me on how to forgive myself, for feeling like a failure for so long.

Major breakthrough number one.

Maria offered to help me further with phone consultations, because being a full-time mum I found it hard to make weekly and fortnightly appointments.

Once again, I couldn't understand why I had to go through this too? When was life going to cut me a break? The contractions would last six hours from the moment I opened my eyes in the morning, until I'd pick up my girls from school, every day. The spasms were always two to five minutes apart. It started to piss me off.

To top it off, I was getting frustrated because I'd stopped writing this book. It just wasn't happening.

I was stuck, and no matter how hard I tried, I couldn't remember the initial cancer diagnosis or the chemo treatments.

How stupid! How could I forget those memories? When I'd try to remember things, there was nothing but a blank canvas in the back of my mind. I'd contracted temporary amnesia.

January 2012

With the uterine pains and contractions intensifying after a few phone consultations and 'normal' counselling sessions, I asked Maria for another session using another technique like the first one. I wanted to experience the exhilaration again. I needed it to work

Maria was aware that I wanted to 'repair' the amnesia of my cancer. She asked me if I would feel comfortable regressing back to the moments of the initial diagnosis and I jumped at the chance. Anything to refresh my memory.

The way Maria took me back to diagnosis was so gentle and non threatening, that I was completely comfortable in the moment. It was in no way traumatic, because I was simply watching the replay of those moments on a theatre screen, in a cinematic visualisation. Even though I felt the similar emotions of those moments, it was safe, because I was detached from actually being there. I was ready to take on my demon. My cancer.

While I was still in the regression, Maria asked my permission to take it a step further. The following is a segment of the transcript from that session.

'What we're going to do at this point is, I'd like you to go into your body and sit beside your body as it's receiving its treatment, as the chemotherapy is going into your body, and into the areas that it needs to go into. I'd like you to sit beside your body, and if you feel comfortable, sit beside the cancer itself. Allow your body and the cancer to speak to you. To tell you from its point of view what it's experiencing. Just in your own time. There's no rush'

I hesitated to do the 'sit beside the cancer,' thing because I hated it. I hated my cancer with my entire being. It had ruined my life. It had destroyed a part of me that I would never get back. I became so incredibly angry at it, so furious I felt my face burn. From the beginning of chemo I had seen the cancer as an evil force. A creature with a wicked grin, invading my body and taking possession of what was not rightfully his to take.

During that moment, I also felt the difficulty and intensity of the treatment. The physical side effects of treatments began sinking into my stomach.

As we went on, I calmed down because I'd had another massive breakthrough. It wasn't my fault. Cancer was not my fault.

I had come to a gentle understanding with myself that my body and I were not to blame. There was no misdemeanour on my part. It hadn't happened because of neglect or poor judgement. I didn't 'deserve' it.

Cancer was not a form of punishment because I'm a terrible person. It just happened for reasons beyond my understanding.

It had taken nearly two years to get to this point, and the burning coal of anger I had been holding disappeared, along with a waterfall of tears. I cried through the entire session.

This was one of the most cathartic experiences I had ever had. Without this session, I would not have been able to heal the anger and the emotional trauma of having cancer that was lying suppressed deep inside my soul. I felt such a tremendous relief because finally I was able to put the actual journey to rest.

Major breakthrough number two.

Although a massive part of the emotional trauma associated with having cancer had been healed, the uterine pains remained. Through more of our phone consultations after the previous session, she gently suggested that for the pain to be present after all the work we had done, there might be repressed trauma that I hadn't touched on.

I didn't know what she was talking about, so Maria gave me time to think about what I needed to process. There was the only more thing left to talk about, but I was so deep in denial that I wasn't ready.

March 2012

I continued with daily life. The excruciating pains would tear through every reproductive part of my body. I couldn't walk. I couldn't speak.

Lowering my pride once more, I went to see Maria, driving hunched over the steering wheel from the continual searing pain. She studied me closely, and because she works intuitively, she knew there was an underlying issue that I had been refusing to talk about.

Rape. The word left my mouth before I could even stop it, almost like I'd spat it out. I had never spoken to anyone about this abuse of my past. Not even my family. No one.

In the first session, talking about being bashed unconscious had been painful but fairly straightforward, because I'd spoken about it many times with my family. Talking about the childhood molestation had been heavier, as my emotions took over with memories resurfacing of trust being broken with people so close to the family, starting from a very young age.

Those were the memories that had always plagued me, and more so during my darker days while in chemotherapy. They had been with me until I'd finished chemo, when I realised I'd let go of the huge weight of them, eventually cutting the final ties through the first therapy sessions.

But the rape was something I'd almost forgotten. Every time I thought back to that part of my past, I'd ignore it and move on with my day, until squashing it down became habit and the memories were non-existent. In my mind, the word 'rape' was in no way connected to me and had never happened.

Taking a deep breath to try and calm down as I relived that part of my past, the tears furiously began cascading down my face and wouldn't stop, but I kept talking. Consumed by shame and guilt for too many years, this was something that I had locked away in the deepest recesses of my mind. I'd felt forced to keep it a secret for so long, that it felt good to finally tell someone I trusted and release it. I needed to get it out of me. To get it off my chest.

With Maria's guidance through this session, I was able to identify the connection of all of my traumas. In every difficult situation, I would always blame myself, and get caught up in a vicious cycle of guilt, self-criticism, disapproval and resentment. I hated myself for always being in the wrong place at the wrong time.

Especially after the rape. I was so disgusted that I had 'allowed' it to happen to me, that self-respect became something so extremely non-existent and long forgotten. Self-value and self-worth also perished with it so long ago, along with trust and child-like innocence.

I would stay in the shower for hours scrubbing my body to try and rid it clean from what had happened. I dealt with it all on my own, because in my mind, it had all been my fault. Many times, I contemplated suicide, because I wasn't worthy of living.

However, during this session, I learnt how to stop and let it go. Let it *all* go. I *wasn't* responsible.

How does anyone deserve to be raped? How does any teenager deserve to be brutally bashed and left for dead? How does a young child deserve to be molested by the people she looks up to and trusts the most? No. *None* of it was my 'fault' and I didn't 'deserve' any of it.

And I was free. Sincerely, genuinely and utterly free. With Maria's gentle navigation, I was able to finally release myself from twenty-one years of emotional scars. Finally.

Major breakthrough number three.

In the follow up session a week later, we had finally made some progress and came to an amazing conclusion.

We connected the pains that had started in April with my parents talking about holidaying overseas. The destination they were going to was where I had been raped. When they mentioned it to me, I remembered the panic and how I'd ignored the memories and the very raw emotions that surfaced.

My terror that they would possibly find out I was raped had somehow triggered the intensifying pain.

And through that last crucial session, the pains had just about disappeared. In order to complete the process, there was only one thing left to do. Tell my family.

During the week I built up the courage (through minor anxiety attacks) and opened up to my family, ready to face them with the news. It was a huge shock to say the least, but it was released. My family stood united beside me and there was not a hint of shame, guilt, anger or blame. Anger maybe, towards the abusers, but not against me.

A week later, I woke up bewildered to no pain. No cramping. Nothing. It was absolutely wonderful to feel total comfort in the area that had been killing me softly for just over eleven months.

February 2013

Upon finishing this book, I received a letter for the long awaited laparoscopy and hysteroscopy. Although the pain was gone, and hadn't been present for almost a year, I needed to see for myself that I had already healed my uterus through those incredible therapy sessions. I took it as a sign that this surgery had been pushed forward from the initial wait time of three to five years.

In spite of everything I've been through already, the mild anxiety attacks in preparation for this type of surgery were unavoidable. The nagging question, 'what if they find something,' disturbed my inner peace.

Joking around with the staff as my usual 'hospital patient' came out to play, the surgery was over before I knew it.

In fact, I sit here at 3:30 a.m., typing with the painful side effect of the gas—a throbbing and winding ache in my chest and right shoulder, excited to share the conclusion: all normal findings in the uterus, ovaries and surrounding area. I did it! This is all the evidence I need!

And I can't help but question: do our bodies react to how we think? Are physical ailments and illnesses a reaction to what goes on in our thoughts or our subconscious, with our supressed or repressed traumas? Is it all psychosomatic?

Did my particular cancer grow in my body due to all the supressed hurt I'd ignored over the years? Maybe it did. Maybe it didn't. That is something I'm not sure of, even though it may make some sense with my personal background. There may be some truth behind cancer growth and emotional suppression/repression in some cases, but not in all.

Was the pelvic pain so strong because of the emotional pain of the rape I had severely repressed? And does the fact that the location of the pain being in my sexual organs have anything to do with rape being sexual abuse?

Spiritually, I know the answer, and believe in my answer, because I have lived through that myself. But then again, not every woman with those types of pains has endured sexual abuse, so it's hard to assume if that was the case.

All I can say is that, for me, healing the emotional trauma by forgiving myself and putting the guilt, self-hatred and self-blame to rest, while connecting it to the physical aspect of myself, released me from physical, emotional, mental and spiritual pain.

Another incredible person I continue to share my journey with, Dr Stephen Opat, spoke to me at a recent appointment about state of mind while battling cancer.

Dr Opat has generously contributed the following:

> There are a number of studies looking at
> the psychological state and cancer outcomes.
> It is quite a controversial area.

Some studies show an association between poor psychological state (mainly depression and pessimism) and cancer survival. This may be due to depressed or pessimistic patients having difficulty adhering to treatment programs.

In addition, patients with more advanced cancer may be more depressed/pessimistic. So their poor outcome may be a reflection of the extent of their disease rather than their psychological state.

With all the medical professionals I've spoken with, what we do believe as a collective, is that the mind is a powerful thing. From the moment I was diagnosed, I had obliviously combined three forms of complementary therapies at different stages of my medical treatments and remission: alternative medicine (traditional Chinese medicine); mind–body intervention (holistic therapies, art therapy, music and dance); and biological based therapies (nutrition). And the one thing that I am absolutely certain of is that combining all of these aspects helped ease my fight.

While I would never dismiss a patients' need for medical intervention, because it *is* crucial to the patient, I do believe that by using an integrative approach, we can expand the boundaries and bring together the best possible treatment to help support our body and mind through treatment, and after treatment. To help treat 'us' as a whole, rather than just focusing on the physical body. Every aspect of our selves needs the same amount of care, especially when fighting for life.

It's a shame that there is so much stigma surrounding alternative therapies—particularly Traditional Chinese medicine and counselling.

When counselling was suggested to me in the beginning of my journey, I dismissed it immediately, because 'I'm fine. I'm not crazy.' There's nothing wrong with my mind, just my body. However, in finding a type of counselling technique I was comfortable with, with someone I completely trusted, and feeling the ease of side-effects from herbs, prescribed from someone else I trusted, and mixing it all up with music and dance while learning how to trust *myself*, I now believe wholeheartedly in the importance of healing the mind, body and soul.

Although I may never forget the traumas of my history, I have made peace with my past.

Liberation is finally mine.

17

THINK OF ALL THE BEAUTY THAT REMAINS

When talking about cancer, there are no winners or losers. There is no right way or wrong way to go about it. Cancer is not a game, or some competition that we've trained for, and it's definitely not something we've agreed to take part in. It's a very real, invasive disease that we can't control or simply push aside to deal with later. There *is* no later.

But the human spirit is so strong, that whatever is thrown at us, we adjust and keep going. No matter how hard the road is and how impossible it looks, we change with it. We may throw a tantrum about it, reaching our wits end about a situation, or scream at the injustice of it, but subconsciously, we don't give up. We can't. We keep going, even if we don't understand how we're doing it at the time. We do whatever we need to do, day by day, to get *through* each day, as best we can.

We may not wear a suit of armour with machine guns strapped to our chests and black war paint smeared on our faces, but to me, going through cancer is still a fight: a fight for what we love—life.

In my life I've made many wrong decisions and countless stupid mistakes. I still do. I've been hurt a thousand times by the people closest to me and learnt many tough lessons. The main lesson is, with everything that happens, it's my choice how I react: whether I choose to be hurt, whether I choose to give up or let things get to me, or whether I choose to forgive myself and walk forward. Because in the end, my choice is always happiness. My choice is peace.

In this world, with so much sadness surrounding us, we seem to sabotage our happiness, like it's too good to be true to feel the slightest hint of joy. For some reason, we feel guilty or not worthy of it. But happiness is already there, within us. It doesn't just come to you like a reward if you're good, and it's not supplied to you by others. It's right there, deep inside the chambers of your heart. And when you finally find it and have it in your grasp, hold onto it. Hold onto it as if your life depends on it, because a life of misery expecting nothing but negativity is a wasted life, and you deserve to be free of that—to be liberated.

In the year of my cancer journey, I was chasing after my life. Cancer didn't care about the pain and havoc it had created for me or my family. It didn't care that I needed to slow down, or take a break from the devastation it had thrown us all in to. It was up to me, and discovering that my mind was more powerful than anything that could happen to me, I kept pushing through.

It was only after fighting for my life and living through pain after pain that I stopped taking everything so seriously. Would I change any of my past? No, because I have a newfound appreciation of who I am.

People watching me going through treatment used to say to me, 'You're so positive all the time. If it was me, I couldn't fight like you. I couldn't do it. I don't know how you do it.' I used to think, do what? I'm not doing anything differently than anyone else in this situation. Because you don't know how strong you are until it's the only choice you have and I had a lot to be strong for.

Having cancer definitely puts things into a different perspective, because life is just too short to sweat the small stuff. I now live day by day, appreciating my life for how wonderful it is and appreciate that every day, I'm still here and I get to live it. Don't get me wrong, I'm far from perfect and my life isn't always peachy—I have my share of bad days too, but they don't last as long as they used to.

There is always the unspoken fear of relapse. That's something I don't think I'll ever escape. There are moments when my body begins to ache and a secret inner paranoia whispers in my subconscious, is it cancer? Is it back?

I then bury that anguish with a smile, because I now believe that I can overcome any challenge thrown my way, choosing to live my life instead of waiting for cancer to come back. Learning to let go of anything unnecessary and focus on what is important in my life is empowering, and something I'm still learning and practise on a daily basis.

I have a new understanding with my body and I've learnt how to listen to it and accept it, adjusting when I need to, especially living with the mild after effects of chemo and radiation.

Some days, I'm forced to rest more than usual, because overpowering fatigue can slow me down. I've learnt to take time out instead of pushing my body beyond its limits, like I used to, because the dizziness and light-headedness that happens from exerting myself just isn't worth it. Even though I'm fairly fit from all the fitness classes I do, my stamina has definitely been altered.

People have little understanding of this type of weakening fatigue and it can be difficult to explain. I may look healthy and normal, and I feel normal, and I act normal (well, some might argue that), but when fatigue strikes, that's my body's way of telling me to stop, breathe and take time out.

My vocal cords have been paralysed because of the size of the tumour. The drastic changes in my voice can be quite entertaining. I'm forever forcing my voice out, having to adjust the volume level I speak at for it to be audible. This can become especially awkward in a Zumba® class, when yelling out to my participants and my voice breaks off, with no one able to hear me. They end up nodding and smiling, pretending to have heard what I've said, with dazed expressions on their faces.

I love my participants.

On the days that I'm tired, my voice tends to disappear. On the rare occasions my voice comes out normally, I have a private celebration. When it breaks into chipmunk, I find myself laughing and shaking my head. People must think I'm crazy, but I no longer care what people think of me. It is what it is and I've embraced my newfound huskiness.

Coughing has become the norm along with mild asthma. I may have to stop to catch my breath more than usual, but it's manageable and easy to live with. I find myself explaining to people that I'm not sick, that I don't have laryngitis or the flu. I've had cancer, and I usually follow that admission with a proud smile.

My left shoulder stiffens and aches in the same area that the PICC line was in and there are certain positions that cause pain in that shoulder. Sometimes I get pins and needles and feel imaginary ants running up and down my left arm to the palms of my hands and fingers. Some days, my hands become numb and I lose strength in my left hand (neuropathy). It freezes involuntarily, becoming rigid and difficult to move, but it usually doesn't last long.

My hair has grown back, with the top of my head curlier than the rest. It makes for an interesting style. At first, it grew back with more grey hairs than what I was used to, but they gradually turned back to their normal colour.

There are moments that I still suffer from the fogginess of chemo brain. My short-term memory has become comical, where I can laugh at myself for forgetting the smallest of things, like misplacing car keys, and losing my phone every five minutes. I've had to resort to writing notes and daily calendar entries to remember the smallest of things.

I watch my diet now, being careful not to consume excess sugar or alcohol. When I do, the area where the tumour once was in my chest begins to throb and my body begins to ache. I am human and have a love affair with food, so I tend to indulge in the occasional cake and cocktails, but I keep it in check with what I've learnt from alkalising foods, and moderate all the good tasting bad stuff. Drinking lots of water tends to help any ache or throb.

There are days that I retain so much fluid I feel like the marshmallow man. A cup of green tea works wonders for it, and usually deflates me back down to my normal self.

The tumour has left residual scar tissue in my chest and it has never felt the same, and probably never will.

Out of all the after effects, the things I have fallen in love with the most are my battle scars. The scarring left over from surgery has been framed proudly with a lymphoma ribbon tattooed around it. I wear that scar along with the chemo stripes around my neck and shoulders and the area on the inside of my arm where my PICC line was taped, with pride. They are all my daily proof of what I can do and how far I can go when I'm pushed.

Sometimes I wish I could be the person who gets up in the morning to a hot steaming cup of strong coffee with a cigarette, but I can't be that person. My body will never return to what it was and I'm okay with that. I've accepted this new normal.

My family have also changed post cancer. They become just as paranoid as me when I get the slightest hint of a headache or pain. Getting a cold sends everyone off into a panic and demands to run to a doctor. It's when they panic that I come to a dead halt, and I can't help but laugh to myself, because the roles reverse and I become their support person, comforting them that I'm fine. It's not cancer, it's a cold. I'm pretty sure the survival rate is high for a runny nose.

The deep-rooted desire I have now is to advocate the importance of lymphoma awareness while articulating the journey as a lymphoma survivor, and if I can help one cancer patient find their own way through it, then my job is done.

Bringing the concept of Liberation™ through dance and music to life for cancer patients would be incredible. To bring back joy and laughter is a dream I wish to unravel with time.

Helping other patients reach their own liberation would give true meaning to my own fight.

My heartfelt sincerity goes out to all the daily survivors fighting for life, before, during and after treatments, because it sucks and is a grave injustice, no matter what age.

My condolences also go out to those who have lost their lives to this horrid disease, and to their families and supporters as well. I couldn't begin to imagine your pain. The fact that you too are living every day through the hurt of losing someone makes you survivors too.

With or without cancer, in the story of life, we all have choices—to live and learn and adjust and change with what is thrown into our path, or to give up. We are all stronger than we give ourselves credit for. Even when in doubt, every day brings with it a clean page. It's up to you how you write it.

Personally, keeping my life balanced in all of its aspects influences inner peace. Maintaining that balance is essential to that peace staying with me. I constantly surround myself with my family. They are my strength and keep me grounded. It's home where I find myself, even through all the noise.

Outside of my family, I still run my classes, which I love with a passion. Happiness has a tendency to explode from inside when I'm teaching. I get to dance and share that joy with others. That is my job, and I couldn't think of a better job to go to. Because it's not just about fitness and weight loss to me. My classes are about losing ourselves to the music, having fun, escaping the monotony of everyday life and creating a party for my participants. That is more important to me than anything else. Combining this passion with raising my family and surrounding myself with only a handful of close friends has been the key to my happiness.

Breaking through the chains of cancer, I celebrate freedom with a cancerversary every year and I will carry the memories with me, always. My cancer *journey* no longer angers me. The guilt and blame have disintegrated. I no longer feel the need to live up to anyone's expectations, including my own, because I deserve a good life. We all do.

Although life can be unfair sometimes, it's still good. Enjoy it. No one is guaranteed tomorrow; that's the harsh truth of life—but, it's never too late to be happy. If anything, always remember that.

Because as Nelson Mandela once said, 'As I walked out the door toward my freedom, I knew that if I did not leave all the anger, hatred, and bitterness behind, I would still be in prison.'

Believe in miracles, because you are one.

18

THE SUPPORTERS

Find arms that will hold you at your weakest
times, eyes that will see your beauty at your ugliest
times, and a heart that will love you at your worst
~ Unknown

During treatment, I refused any photos my family and friends wanted to take of me. Many times Paul wanted to film me having chemo, to record the memories so I could look back later at the struggles, the pain and the achievements of my life with cancer. He also wanted the memories for himself and our children.

Although the memories are engraved in my mind, I regret not having something more to look at and watch, as unbelievable or stupid as that may sound.

My family were my pillar of strength through the duration of my treatment. Not only did I adapt to this new life as a cancer patient, they adjusted too. As a family, we were quick to modify our lives with each crossroad we came to and we did it together.

Each time we were forced down a new path, no matter how bleak or chaotic it was, it became our new way of life. They pulled me through it everyday with the smallest things they could do to help.

My mum felt guilty that she had to work, so she would have the kids' lunches ready and packed and lay their breakfasts out on the kitchen bench every morning before school. After taking my daughters to school, my father would take Jaivan off my hands for a couple of hours, allowing me time to rest or nap. He would feed him, play with him and keep him entertained, giving me time to heal, reflect and focus on myself.

Paul would arrive home in the early evening after work and take the kids to the backyard and play with them until it was dark. I loved watching them all together. I love that memory. I wouldn't let him take them to the park. It was healing for me to hear them all laughing and screaming, to be surrounded by all of them all the time, even if all I could do was just lie on the couch to watch.

My daughters worked out that when mama was on the couch with the dark circles under her eyes and the bucket on the floor, meant quiet playtime. They would steal off to their bedrooms and play together.

Occasionally they would come out, throw their arms around me and shower me with kisses and tell me how much they loved me. Before heading back to their rooms, Aaliyah would turn around and say, 'Mama, I'm proud you're my mama,' which would tear me to pieces on the inside. They kept me going. They were my strength.

Not a day went by that I didn't give thanks for my family and friends. I had an amazing support team.

While my family and few close friends were strong around me, I lost a few other friends in the process. Eventually, I stopped analysing and judging people and their reactions for my own peace of mind.

Cancer is a transformative experience for everyone. The changes around you can be difficult to swallow and can hit you like the seasons, but you keep going and eventually let it go.

You may find that you lose some friends on the way and make new ones through treatment, only to find you lose others once you hit remission.

Some people will show so much sudden interest in you while undergoing treatment, even people you haven't heard from in years, only to lose interest when it's over. What they don't realise, is that it's never truly over.

Don't let that bring you down. Everyone has their own way of dealing with trauma, and in the case of cancer, it can be traumatic for everyone involved.

Most people don't know what to say, how to approach you, or what is a safe topic to talk about. While all we crave is normal conversation, and to be treated as the person we are and not for what we have, most people find that hard to grasp. It's hard not to question or analyse where we went wrong, or what role we played—if any—in their decision to leave when we need them the most. At times it can be bittersweet.

However, having said that, I have dear friends that were living through personal traumas of their own during the time of my journey and they have recently come back into my life. We all move on at some point. Not everyone is necessarily bad for leaving your side. It's important to remember that. Don't dismiss people entirely. Only time will tell.

While we are going through our personal hell, our loved ones are going through the same amount of turmoil and suffering, if not more, just by watching us. They may not show it or react the way we expect them to, but they are. I never knew what was really going on behind closed doors with my family. Only upon finishing this book, did they tell me their own experiences as cancer supporters.

Because it was a fight from the soul, for all of them too.

Here are some of their words:

Paul

I was lost. I didn't know what to do or how to help you through it. All I wished was that somehow I could have controlled it in someway, to stop it from hurting you, but I didn't know how and I couldn't. I felt helpless.

All the way through, it hurt me to watch you go through it, because I had no idea what cancer was all about, and I wanted more than anything to take it away from you. As I went through it with you, I learnt about what it was that you were living through. How you handled it amazed me. I couldn't imagine going through it myself, watching how you suffered with your symptoms and the changes I saw in you.

The thought of losing you scared me. That's why I held on to you more, and became closer to you. I love you so much, I felt sorry for you, that you had to go through that. You're too young to face something like that. When you went through your dark days, so did I, and I didn't stop worrying until they mentioned remission.

The second time, when we broke down crying together, I thought that was it. That it was more aggressive and I'd lose you.

You know now I look at you sometimes and I can't believe you're here with me. I can't believe I can still touch you and talk to you and laugh with you. I know if things went different, you wouldn't be here with me now. I love that I can still look at you, still hold you close to me. I love you.

Dad

I prayed every night for you to come out of that bitter moment, and I asked God and begged Him to help you.

When Mel came to get you to take you to the needle biopsy, I cried watching you leave, scared for your life, scared for what you would find. I couldn't show you how desperate I was feeling to have you healthy and back to normal. I was afraid for you.

When you were leaving for your major surgery, I was distressed and heavy hearted, worried because it was so close to your heart with vessels wrapped around your tumour. When you told me how Professor Choong prayed for you, so that God could guide his hands to be able to find answers to save you, it profoundly reached my soul. That was incredible. We owe that man everything.

The moment you told me it was confirmed that you had cancer for me was a huge shock. It was an enormous concern and worry everyday at every moment. Scared for you and of the actual disease and what it was doing to you. Scared for your children, my grandchildren. When you admitted to me how scared you were, as your father, I felt so sorry and deeply saddened for what you had to endure. It wasn't fair to see you like that.

All I could do was think about you, and what you must have been feeling.

Watching my daughter and seeing your health deteriorate so fast, hurt me to no end.

It was a wonderful surprise when they told you it was gone. I thanked God that He listened to my prayers.

Your mother and I feel enormous gratitude for Dr Raj, Professor Choong, and Dr Louis Cali. The three guardians sent to you to help you survive and gain back your life.

Mum

When you first called me and told me that you had a tumour in your chest, I didn't know what to do, I didn't know what to say. All I could do was cry. I remember telling you, 'Don't worry, we can beat it, we can all fight it.' But when we finished that conversation, I went straight to my boss and I just fell apart. I broke. I said to her, 'Why? She doesn't deserve this? She hasn't done anything wrong to anybody?'

I felt that you were being punished, and my biggest question was why.

It wasn't easy, Karina. It was hard, because no mother wants to see her child sick like that. No mother. It's a very difficult thing to swallow, it's like, it's like there's no answer to the questions, and then I said to God, 'Why did you give it to her? Give it to *me* instead. She has three little kids. She *needs* to raise them.'

Watching you leave for the surgery, I was extremely anxious, nervous and scared. All I could do was pray and be there one hundred per cent for your babies. One day I was driving to work and I used to talk to God a lot in the car. But I called on Mother Mary, pleading with her, 'Virgin Mary, you were a mother and you lost a son. You need to help me. You know how it feels.' And then I said, 'I know with your help, she's going to come out of this. She's going to beat it. This cancer doesn't belong there. That cancer does not belong in that chest. Karina does not deserve it.'

I used to cry on the way to work, and on the way home. But work was the place where I could cry as much as I needed to before going home to see you.

It was very difficult holding my strength in front of you, and it was even harder to watch you getting all the chemo into your body. It was painful for me to see you go through all that. My wish that it would be over quick, and I just wanted to know that everything was working and that bastard was going to leave you alone.

I rang our family in Colombia and everybody started praying for you there too.

The day you called me that the tumour was shrinking, was the happiest day of my life, like taking a breath of fresh air, because I knew it was going to be beaten.

The second time around, I felt like a ton of bricks had fallen on me, when I heard your voice telling me crying that it had come back, but at the same time, I said in my head, 'If she beat it the first time, she can do it a second time.'

Now, I admit, sometimes I feel like I'm living on the edge. I get scared when you tell me you feel something different in your body. I too fear relapse for you. I don't want to see you go through that again. To see you fight just to be alive.

But, I feel extremely relieved and happy, and blessed that you are here, because I could never imagine my life without you. Never. Knowing that I would have your children with me, I could never do it without you. I'm very proud of you, and for what you're doing for other patients. For bringing your voice out, for letting them know how it is, for sharing your truth. Because something good came out of something evil. That's what I'm sure of. I know in my heart that this book is going to help a lot of people.

Dr Raj (Dr D Rajesperasingam)

I can still remember the day Karina walked into my office. It was about two years ago, and she had been experiencing some chest symptoms that had been persisting for a few weeks. We decided on a chest X-ray. When the results arrived all I could think about was how I was going to break the news to her. I could sense the tension she held during the conversation over the phone but I preferred to tell her in person.

She arrived at the clinic in minutes, her face with a mixture of emotions. My fear at that moment was of how she was going to take the news. I looked at her, and indicated to the reports I was holding. This was followed by a short silence. She was waiting for my next words. When I told her they found a tumour, she was in tears. I remember her reaction. 'Dr Raj, am I going to die?' I reassured her that we didn't know yet, but we had a lot of investigating to do. I knew that Karina could fight, and that she would fight.

The story here in her book has been written honestly and openly. As I mentioned above, Karina fought, and she succeeded. With the combination of her strong will, medical treatment, and the support she received from family and friends, she defeated the cancer.

Karina's life is not just a story, but also the journey of a strong, determined woman who knew that her every effort would be with positive results. Now Karina is more active than before.

Liberation is a must read book, especially those encountering the same or a similar situation. *Liberation* will inspire others to fight for life.

19

S UR-VI-VOR—NOUN [SER-VAHY-VER]: A PERSON WHO CONTINUES TO FUNCTION OR PROSPER IN SPITE OF OPPOSITION, HARDSHIP, OR SETBACKS

The world boxes us into four walls of pity and sorrow, with the title of 'victim' and 'poor you' written in thick black ink, judging us, not knowing what cancer is really all about. For most of us, we want to tear down those walls and recreate mind-blowing lives, regardless of our situations. The journey to discovering the new you can be just as daunting.

While on the ride, I used to say, 'I'm not dead. I'm still here and I want to have fun while I can.' Because it

was never about feeling sorry for myself. That's not what any of us are about, despite how the world sees us.

When people tell you to think positive, little do they know that you already are. Even though you're facing a life-threatening illness with no return ticket and no way out, you keep going, living through it daily, weekly, monthly, yearly. That is being positive.

When people tell you to be strong, what does that mean? Your strength is already doubling every day. Especially when you feel weak and defeated, falling to pieces on the inside, keeping a smile on your face when you feel like breaking. Every moment of every day that you're living in this seemingly never ending journey is where you find your strength.

It's not about hiding the anger, the anguish, the heartache, the frustration, the fear, the suffering, the impatience, the confusion, the darkness, the injustice, the mourning of your former life or the confusion of finding your new life.

Because you're allowed to do all of that and more and anyone that tells you otherwise has no understanding of life as a cancer patient.

It's about living every moment, one minute, one hour and one day at a time. If you have something to say, say it. If you feel like throwing something against the wall, do it. If you need to cry and scream, go for it. If you feel like flying into laughing hysterics, fly into it!

You'll feel so much better for releasing any of the emotions you're feeling, even if it only lasts a short moment. Embrace the person you are and how you're dealing with it, and eventually it becomes easier to accept the journey you are living.

Keep digging for answers. Don't give up *your* right to heal yourself, both mentally and spiritually. Trust and believe in yourself, because it could very well influence your physical body. After all, you only have one vessel to live in. Take care of it, nurture it, with whatever you're most comfortable with. A distraction in the form of a hobby or a favourite pastime can be just as important, taking the edge off your fight. Throughout treatment or years later, it's never too late to start.

Acknowledge the changes, both the physical with the emotional, while strengthening your will to live. After all, most things in life are not permanent. It's what you make it. Give it everything you have and create as many beautiful memories as you can, not only for some peace of mind for yourself, but for your family and friends. Every memory you create will live on indefinitely through someone's tears and another's laughter.

Whatever you decide to do, make sure it makes you happy.

You are not your cancer, you are you. Leave behind that legacy.

To someone, you are a hero, whether you like it or not. Even through your so-called weakest moments. You don't know the extent of how many people you can touch with inspiration. To us, it's just our story. It's just something we had to do while we were doing it. To most of us it's no big deal. However, to people around us, we are an amazing group of people.

Sometimes I still have moments of bewilderment and awe that I went through what I did. It's something you never think will happen to you, until it does.

Someone once said to me that I am nothing without cancer, that I use cancer to hide behind, and that I will never amount to anything without it. It's only cancer, and I lived, so I should simply just 'get over it.' The arrogance of some people will never cease to amaze me—close-minded simply because they have not walked in my shoes, felt what I have felt, or seen what I have seen.

To these people I must say back that I am everything because of my cancer. How can one hide behind something that has become a part of their DNA? Yes, even though my cancer is gone, it remains a part of me and I will live with the remnants of it every day for the rest of my life.

If it wasn't for my cancer journey, I wouldn't have formed a loving relationship with my body. I wouldn't have found the self-respect and self-worth that I deserved for so long, yet continually denied myself. I wouldn't have let go of past pains and trauma that needed to be let go of.

I wouldn't be passionate about raising lymphoma awareness as I am now, giving it a voice, because we deserve just as much respect and go through just as much hell as other types of cancers.

Decades of research may have improved survival, but sadly, not everyone survives.

I wouldn't have created the concept for Liberation™ to help other patients find alleviation through health, dance and music. I wouldn't have met all the beautiful people that shared my journey with me, or rediscovered hope in humanity through the amazing and selfless acts of others in this human race.

I wouldn't have discovered the magical relief of herbs or become passionate about traditional Chinese medicine supporting and working with conventional medicine. I wouldn't have faith that emotional trauma may be connected to physical ailments, or have been the guinea pig, unknowingly testing these theories out for myself.

I wouldn't have made the crucial changes I have made in my life, or have formed an unbreakable bond with my husband and my family. I wouldn't have found the true meaning of my life and feel what it is like to be really alive, because I didn't just survive—I learnt how to live.

Nobody can tell you how you should feel or what you should do. Especially when you've had your life planned out in a picture perfect vision of how it's all going to be, and then you feel like Hurricane Cancer tears through your plans, blowing your life into the wind and leaving a path of destruction for you to clean up along with aftershocks of fear.

Before cancer, I didn't really care about the disease, because I had no understanding of it. In the beginning I knew nothing about cancer, completely innocent to the fiery dragon it can be and oblivious to the harm it can cause. All I knew was the more knowledge I had, the better and more in control I felt. A doctor doesn't know your body the way you know it. Only you know how you feel. Your body is yours.

When I go in to the hospital for my check ups, the hospital smell still turns my stomach but then I look around and sometimes force myself to look down the hallway at the chemo ward, thanking God I no longer have to be in there hooked up to machines and cables.

I've seen the children who are also fighting, and I've spoken to parents who have lost their babies to this disease. The injustice many people face daily is infuriating.

I know it could have ended differently for me, and having nine more years of remission ahead of me makes it all the more real. The world needs to recognise that lymphoma is cancer, it's not just some random disease.

Sometimes I look back and wonder why any of us have to battle cancer. After much soul searching, I don't really know the answer. Maybe it's about creating a change, or a difference to others surrounding us, no matter how small we think those changes are. Maybe it's about learning more about ourselves, about life, and believing that we can do anything we put our minds to.

No matter how bleak the outcome can be, we are all survivors, because from the moment of diagnosis, a survivor is born. Even when we're think we're not built for something like cancer, we can get through it. Even in our weakest moments, we find our strength. Even when we're being battered and bruised internally, suffering emotional whiplash from the never-ending storms and darkness, we stay afloat. Even when we think we can't, we can.

The smallest things can change your life in a blink of an eye. It sets you on a path that you never imagined into a future you never envisioned. And sometimes, you have to step into the blinding darkness and walk through it for a while in order to find your light, whatever that means to you.

The reality is, cancer is still an arsehole, and it will probably always be to me. I don't think that will ever change for most of us. However, I am thankful for my journey, for having an amazing path to walk, and showing me what it did. For meeting all of the incredible survivors I met and continue to meet. For pushing me to become who I am, showing me that there is life after cancer and for enlightening me with gratitude for my life.

For all of that and more, I thank you.

THE LYMPHATIC SYSTEM

The following information and diagram was extracted from the patient booklet *Understanding Hodgkin Lymphoma—A guide for patients and families* with the generous permission of the Leukaemia Foundation.

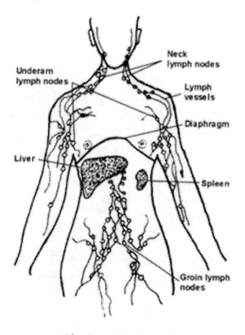

The Lymphatic System

Summary

The lymphatic system is a made up of a vast network of lymph vessels that branch out into all the tissues of the body. The two main roles of the lymphatic system are: to drain excess fluid from the body's tissues, filter it and return it to the blood stream; and to harbour specialist white blood cells—lymphocytes—to help fight infection.

Lymph is filtered through filtering organs; the spleen, the thymus and lymph nodes, before being emptied into the blood.

Clusters of small lymph nodes (also known as lymph glands) are found at various points throughout the lymphatic system. These glands act as important filtering stations, cleaning the lymph fluid as it passes through them. Your throat, armpits, chest, abdomen and groin contain these small bean-shaped organs/glands located close to our arteries. Bacteria becomes trapped in the lymph node once it's passed through the tissues by the lymph and the lymphocytes can then remove and destroy the bacteria. This is the reason your lymph nodes tend to swell if you have an infection. Lymph nodes also trap viruses and cancer cells.

Some common lymphatic problems may include glandular fever, oedema (excess swelling caused by fluid), tonsillitis, and lymphoma (Hodgkin and non-Hodgkin).

What is lymphoma?

Leukaemia, lymphoma, myeloma and related blood disorders can develop in anyone, of any age, at any time. Around 11,500★ Australians are expected to be newly diagnosed this year—equivalent to 31 people each day.

Lymphomas are cancers that affect the lymphatic system. Lymphomas arise when developing lymphocytes (a type of white blood cell) undergo a malignant change and multiply in an uncontrolled way. Increasing numbers of abnormal lymphocytes, called lymphoma cells accumulate and form collections of cancer cells called tumours in lymph nodes (glands) and other parts of the body. Over time, lymphoma cells replace normal lymphocytes, weakening the immune system's ability to fight infection.

Types of lymphomas

There are many different types of lymphoma which are broadly divided into two main groups:

Hodgkin lymphoma (also known as Hodgkin disease) and all other types of lymphoma, which are grouped together and called B-cell or T-cell lymphomas (also known as non-Hodgkin lymphomas).

Incidence

Each year in Australia, around 4300 people are diagnosed with lymphoma★ making it the fifth most common cancer in Australia (sixth most common type of cancer in men and the fifth most common type of cancer in women). Of these, at least 89% of these people have non-Hodgkin's lymphoma.

Lymphomas are seen in all age groups but are more common in people aged 50+. The peak age for diagnosis of Hodgkin Lymphoma is between 15 and 30 years.

Causes

The incidence of lymphoma is increasing every year. In most cases we don't know what causes lymphomas but there are likely to be a number of factors involved. Like all cancers, lymphomas may result from damage to (or mutation of) special proteins called genes that control the growth and division of cells. We know that people with a weakened immune system (either due to an immunodeficiency disease or drugs that suppress the function of the immune system) are at an increased risk of developing lymphomas. Certain types of viral infections may also play a role, especially in people with a weakened immune system.

Symptoms

Lymphomas commonly present as a firm painless swelling of a lymph node (swollen glands), usually in the neck, under the arms or in the groin. Other symptoms may include:

- recurrent fevers
- excessive sweating at night
- unintentional weight loss

- persistent lack of energy
- generalised itching.

Lymphoma may develop in the lymph nodes in deeper parts of the body like those found in the abdomen (causing bloating), or in the chest (causing coughing, discomfort in the chest and difficulty breathing).

In some cases people don't have any troubling symptoms and the disease is picked up during a routine chest X-ray.

Treatment

Treatment will vary depending on the exact type of lymphoma a person has, and how fast it is likely to grow and cause problems in the body. It will also depend on the extent of disease at diagnosis, the person's age and their general health.

Some lymphomas grow slowly and cause few troubling symptoms, and may not need to be treated urgently. Others grow more quickly and need to be treated as soon as they are diagnosed.

The main treatments are chemotherapy and radiotherapy. This is given to destroy the leukemic cells and allow the bone marrow to function normally again. Other types of treatment are also used.

Occasionally, a stem cell transplant is given to treat disease which has relapsed (come back), or where there is a high likelihood that the disease will relapse in the future.

Projections sourced from the Australian Institute of Health and Welfare (AIHW). Estimates are calculated using actual diagnoses data collected from 2007 and annually prior to this year.

Sources

AIHW (2005) Cancer Incidence Projections for Australia 2002-2011

Australian Institute of Health and Welfare and Australian Associated Cancer Registry (2004) Cancer in Australia 2001

The Leukaemia Foundation website
http://www.leukaemia.org.au/web/aboutdiseases/
lymphomas_index.php

THE ALCHEMY OF LIBERATION™

Nutrition and illness

Written by Dr Louis Cali, Registered Acupuncturist and Chinese Herbal Medical Practitioner (VIC); Diplomat in Acupuncture and Chinese Herbal Medicine (NCCAOM); Member of AACMA; VCAT Tribunal Member; Clinical Supervisor RMIT for Chinese Medicine:

With Karina, we discussed diet and the significance of food in dealing with cancer. With the lymph system, foods that are 'damp' and 'phlegm' forming (in a Chinese Medicine sense) are more likely to create stagnation or blockage in the flow of substances in that system. Any blockage or slow-down in movement of vital substances—such as lymph—in the body can lead to problems, like pre-cancerous conditions.

Keeping your diet 'clean,' that is, eating wholesome, fresh, unprocessed foods, is more conducive to health that highly processed foods, which are pro-inflammatory and prone to glug-up the system. The lymph system is particularly susceptible to 'dampness', which causes a more systemic sluggishness in the body.

The 'acid–alkaline' balance reflects the effect of inflammation in the body. The more inflammation through an acid-forming diet, the more a pro-cancer environment is created. Our modern food supply is largely pro-inflammatory, with chronic illness on the rise.

Acid-forming foods, for example highly processed foods and other 'unwholesome' foods like sugar, white wheat, packaged goods, processed foods, all create a pro-inflammatory effect and an acidic environment in the body.

However, alkaline foods or an anti-inflammatory diet reduces inflammation. Whole foods, natural, and fresh foods tend to be anti-inflammatory or neutral in nature. This is an over simplification of course. Through stress reduction, a 'clean' diet and medicine/herbs/nutriceuticals, an internal environment less conducive to the development of cancer can be attained.

Traditional Chinese herbs

In light of the global health crisis, complementary and alternative medicine are becoming increasingly significant, especially the role of traditional Chinese medicine. Integrating Chinese medicine into mainstream health care is becoming a global phenomenon with healthcare beginning to recognise the crucial benefits of herbs.

Traditional Chinese medicine (TCM) is the oldest continuously practiced medicine in the world. It has been refined and perfected over countless generations of doctors for over two and a half millennia.

In all cases, I take an integrative approach to treating cancer, complementing the proposed conventional medical treatment devised by the oncologists with the benefits of Chinese Medicine (herbal medicine and acupuncture).

Chinese herbs have immeasurable benefits for patients combating serious illnesses, malignancy and metastasis, while boosting general health and immunity.

New discoveries into the anti-cancer properties of herbs are being uncovered frequently.

It is my experience, the use of Chinese herbal formulae for patients undergoing chemotherapy invariably improves their comfort level and quality of life. Karina's experience with these herbs is typical, regardless of the type of cancer involved. I have consistently heard similar results from breast cancer patients, leukaemia patients, and bowel cancer patients that the herbs have significantly supported these patients throughout their treatment.

The herbs such as Huang Qi (Astragalus membranaceus), Dang Shen (Codonopsis pilosula) and Chen Pi (Citri reticulatae Pericarpium), tonify and regulate the Qi, or vital energy, and Ji Xue Teng (Spatholobus suberectus), Dang Gui (Angelica sinensis) and Yu Jin (Curcuma longa), tonify and move the blood. They work to keep the digestive system strong.

Other herbs were designed to counteract the toxic effects of the chemo. Liver herbs protect the liver and help it work better to process the toxic chemicals. Some of these herbs clear away heat (reduce inflammation); others to stop pain (by reducing inflammation and improving circulation).

There are different formulae developed for particular types and stages of cancer. I use a variety of approaches to keep cancer patients strong.

For Karina, two formulae were devised. The first or main formula was specifically for lymphoma. It was designed to keep the immune system strong, and clear the accumulated toxic heat resultant from the cancer. Many of these herbs benefit the Lungs and assist in clearing away phlegm. It contained:

Lymphoma formula

Ban lan gen—Isatidis/Baphicacanthis Radix: Clears heat, relieves toxicity, clears damp-heat (infections). For fevers, swellings, pain

Di jin cao—Herba Euphorbiae Humifusae: Clears heat, relieves toxicity, promotes circulation of blood, drains dampness.

Lian qiao—Forsythiae Fructus: Clears heat, relieves toxicity, anti-pyretic (anti-fever), anti-inflammatory.

Tian hua fen—Trichosanthis Radix: Transforms phlegm-heat (created from infections with phlegm present)

Xuan shen—Scrophularia ningpoensis: Clears heat, cools the blood (deep systemic inflammation)

Tu fu ling—Similacis glabrae rhizoma: Clears heat, relieves toxicity, drains damp (corrects the fluid metabolism in the body).

Tu bei mu—Fritillariae thunbergia bulbus: Clears heat, relieves toxicity, dissolves nodules. For swellings, anti-tumoural.

Shan dou gen—Menispermi rhizoma: Clear heat, relieve toxicity, clears damp-heat (clears infection). For swellings, anti-viral.

Niu bang zi—Fructus Arctii: Clears heat, relieves toxicity, releases the exterior (helps move pathogenic influences from the interior to the exterior of the body). For fevers and swellings.

Lu gen—Phragmitis rhizoma: Clears heat, transforms phlegm (break up phlegm), anti-cancer properties.

Gua lou pi—Trichosanthes kirilowii.: Clears heat, transforms phlegm-heat (break up phlegm from an infection), dissipates nodules.

Chuan bei mu—Fritillariae cirrhosae bulbus: Clears heat, transforms phlegm-heat, dissolves nodules.

Each of these herbs have similar actions, all of which work together to tackle a different aspect of the overall problem.

The second formula, called the chemo formula, was designed to protect her system from the toxic effects of the chemotherapy drugs without interfering with their action. The Chemo formula strongly tonifies Qi and Blood, to protect the immune system and essential vital substances. It also nourishes the Yin, which is an aspect of the body that is typically damaged by chemotherapy. It also has medicinals to keep Qi and Blood moving, and clear away toxic heat which also accumulates while undergoing chemo.

It is important to note that this formula was not designed to replicate or replace Karina's chemotherapy treatment devised by her oncologist, or haematologist, but rather support her while undergoing chemotherapy.

Chemo formula

Huang qi—Astragalus membranaceus: Strengthens Qi (or the body's ability to adapt to constant change). A strong immune-boosting effect, helps body produce blood, anti-inflammatory and anti-oxidant effects.

Dang shen—Codonopsis pilosula: Strengthens Qi (or the body's ability to adapt to constant change). A strong immune-boosting effect, helps body produce blood, anti-inflammatory and anti-oxidant effects.

Chen pi—Citri reticulatae Pericarpium: Regulates energy flow in body, dries dampness, transforms phlegm.

Ji xue teng—Spatholobus suberectus: Promotes blood circulation and strengthens blood, stops pain.

Dang gui—Angelica sinensis: Strengthens blood, invigorates blood, stops pain.

Tian men dong—Asparagi radix. Strengthens the Yin aspect of the body—the substance and fluids. Generates fluids, clears heat, anti-fever.

Mai men dong—Ophiopogonis japonicas radix: Strengthens the Yin aspect of the body—the substance and fluids. Generates fluids, clears heat, anti-fever.

Bai hua she she cao—Oldenlandia diffusa: Clears heat, drains fire, relieves toxicity. For swellings, clears damp-heat, anti-tumoural.

Jin yin hua—Lonicerae flos: Clears heat, relieves toxicity, for swellings and fevers. Anti-microbial.

Nu zhen zi—Ligustri lucidi fructus: Nourushes the Liver and Kidneys, clears deficient heat (from Yin deficiency—chronic inflammation)

Yu jin—Curcuma longa: Strong anti-cancer and anti-tumour properties. Promotes blood and Qi circulation, clears heat, reduces inflammation and pain.

Again these herbs work in tandem to help keep the body strong while undergoing chemotherapy.

This is an approach I often used with cancer patients undergoing chemotherapy—a formula designed to support their fight against a specific type of cancer, and another to support them through the side-effects of chemo.

The same approach is used when patients are undergoing radiotherapy, the difference being the herbs used in the radiotherapy formula being ones that specifically deal with side-effects unique to that type of treatment.

Once patients go into remission, herbs should continue to be taken to help keep the immune system strong and operating effectively.

Acupuncture

An important part of cancer support using Chinese medicine is acupuncture. This was certainly true in Karina's case, and has proven to be so with most of the cancer patients I see.

A healthy immune system requires good production of blood, a process that is significantly hampered by cancer and cancer treatment. Acupuncture increases production of white blood cells leading to an increased immune response. Acupuncture also reduces inflammation—a common phenomenon associated with tumour growth, chemotherapy and radiation therapy. With less inflammation, there is less pain and dysfunction.

HOLISTIC COUNSELLING

Written by Maria Kafaltis, Bachelor of Holistic Counselling; Diploma Transpersonal Counselling; Diploma Holistic Counselling; Calm abiding meditation teacher; Reiki practitioner Level II; Member of AAHTC

Treating any patient with a life threatening illness is always a process that must be dealt with, with sensitivity, compassion and honesty. The client will most likely be experiencing the physical demands of chemotherapy and radiation. This alone is cause for great emotional and mental distress.

Holistic counselling is a gentle and compassionate form of therapy that may help the client to help themselves when they feel the need for support or assistance. Holistic counselling approaches disease and disorders as parts of a greater whole. Rather than treating just the symptoms, holistic counselling looks deeper in order to uncover underlying causes. Holistic counselling looks at the interconnectedness of the body, mind and spirit to help facilitate wellness.

Holistic counselling can assist in:

- greater self-awareness and self-acceptance
- a more peaceful, balanced approach to life
- increased health and vitality
- emotional well being
- a deepened sense of spirituality
- a greater ability to cope with traumas such as death, divorce and abuse
- an enhanced feeling of optimism and self-esteem.

The role of the holistic counsellor is to support the client on their journey and assist them in creating a map to navigate that journey, helping them to gain understanding and healing. The holistic counsellor is able to do this via the use of a variety of techniques, some of which include focussing, regression, and art therapy.

Regression

Presenting complaints like fears, depression, sexual problems, personality problems like passivity, or negative convictions like 'it's all my fault,' have causes in the past. The same is true for many physical complaints.

Regression therapy does not analyse the relationship someone has with others, but rather explores the defining moments of that relationship. Regression therapy unlocks the intuitive powers of the client without diminishing in any way their rationality. It works with emotions and bodily sensations and with the mind as well. It avoids sensationalism and fantasy. It has a detective attitude. It tries to be factual and empirical.

Gestalt techniques, Inner Child work, bio-energetic interventions, and rational–emotive therapy are commonly used in Regression therapy. What binds all these techniques together is regression: the liberating discovery and healing of concrete and specific past experiences and their mental, emotional and physical aftermath.

Focussing

Focusing is a form of inward bodily attention. Focusing offers a new way of being with ourselves, that has all of us in it.

Focusing is an interface of body-mind and consists of specific steps for getting a body sense of how you are in a particular life situation. To do this, first we must pause. We need to pause to really notice what our bodies are carrying for us. The body sense is often unclear and vague at first, but if you pay attention it will open up into words or images and you experience a felt shift in your body. This gentle unfolding of the body's wisdom is what is known as Focusing.

In the process of Focusing, one experiences a physical change in the way that the issue is being lived in the body. We learn to live in a deeper place than just thoughts or feelings. We are opened up to the deeper river that runs through us. When we do this our issues look and feel different and new solutions arise.

Art therapy

Art therapy is a form of expressive therapy that uses the creative process of making art to improve a person's physical, mental, and emotional well-being. The expression of oneself creatively and artistically can help people to resolve issues as well as develop and manage their behaviours and feelings, reduce stress, and improve self-esteem and awareness. Artistic talent is not required. The art therapist works with the client to delve into the underlying messages that are communicated through art.

Art therapy works differently with different people. It can be used to externalise situations that the client may find too traumatic or confronting to express verbally. Therefore, it is a wonderful therapy to use with victims of sexual or physical abuse.

ACKNOWLEDGEMENTS AND RECOGNITIONS

I am forever grateful to the following VIPs that followed me on my journey, before, during and after. You all make me believe in the human race again.

Paul. My husband. My rock. For holding me up when I was barely standing. For all the love you shower me with everyday. For the way you look into my eyes, with or without hair, through sickness and in health, and helping me believe in myself again. For blessing me with you as a soul mate and giving me the greatest gifts, our children. You taught me all the lessons about life before I lived them. My heart, you hold, indefinitely. I love you an amazing amount.

My children. I love you all big much. You saved me from myself. You gave me the reason to fight and you give me the reason to keep going. Always. For you. I will never stop loving you.

My parents. The most amazing people I know. I only wish to become the incredible extraordinary human beings you are. Thank you for walking every road I've ever walked, beside me. For holding my hand and never giving up on me. For pushing me everyday to share my story, and believing in me through my whole life journey. For being there to share the silence, and lifting me beyond the stars. For giving me the best moments and creating wonderful memories of laughing until everything hurts. For being the best of best friends anyone could ever ask for. I carry a piece of you both everywhere I go and will forever strive to reach the level of perfection you both are to me. I love you.

Mel. You were my voice when I couldn't speak, and helped me escape when the world became too loud. Thank you for shoving sense into my head the many times I'd lost it. For providing the best entertainment when I needed it. Your support from the beginning was crucial, offering your friendship when I needed it the most. For playing second mum to my babies and helping them forget. For getting your green marker pen out, filling in the gaps, and helping me with this book.

Bec, for being there when I couldn't, last minute, for my babies. For your support and undying faith that I'd kick its ass, and your non-judgmental friendship. For playing third mum to my kids and offering them your house and your kids too. Thank you.

Tracy, my hair and I are forever indebted to your selfless friendship and support. You took care of me at a point that I thought I wasn't worthy.

Adele, quite simply, for being you, and for helping me find me. Cheers to more!

Maria, my beautiful friend, thank you for all of your invaluable guidance, love and support. For helping me through it all from the very beginning. For all of the valuable lessons you've taught me, and most of all, for helping me reach my own personal liberation. I couldn't have done it without you. There will never be enough words, or enough thank yous, for how much you helped me. With Cienna until we are old and senile.

To Patti (with an 'i' not a 'y') for being my vatoness, my mofoness, and every other ness there is. For our chicano u-turns and friendship. Thank you for helping me see the light, guiding me back to what's important. Here's to opening more curtains, creating more memories, laughing til our cheeks hurt, and running out of cleanser. Que reeco!

Dr Raj. You listened to me. You believed in me the whole way, even when I didn't. Thank you for kick starting this crazy ride. For bringing humanity back to the medical system. Thank you for being the wonderful doctor you are. You were and still are a boulder of support for my whole family.

Professor Choong. Thank you for loving your work. For changing the course of my journey for the better. For being there when others refused. For your humbleness and sincerity and faith. I owe you my life.

Dr Louis Cali. You're some kind of all right, even though you're from Philly. This girl from Queens appreciates your intelligence, your sense of humour and your expert advice. Thank you for alleviating my treatments and for sharing your extensive knowledge in this book.

To Dr Opat, thank you for believing in this book and helping me describe the medical aspects perfectly. Your advice is always greatly appreciated!

The Leukaemia Foundation, for your continued support, your patience and for sharing in my vision.

Beautiful Taea. The littlest things mean the most. Thank you for your advice and encouragement. No more doubts. A promise I make to you and myself.

Zumba® and the Zumba Fitness logos are trademarks of Zumba Fitness, LLC, used under license.

$\mathcal{P}$HOTO ALBUM

One month before diagnosis with my babies 2009

Morphine high post needle biopsy

Blackstreet with Paul

Mel and I—4 months into chemo

World's greatest shave

'I love you baby, even without hair'—Paul and I

Waiting for radiation with Paul

From left Me, Mel, Tracy and Paul—after radiation on
one of our nights out, smashing the town

With my three angels—you saved me

Craziness; From left Mel, Me and Adele

Group shot!—amazing group of women; From left:
Julie, Tracy, Nicole, Trudi, Bec, Tracey, Mel, Me

Dress ups with Patti

Maria and I celebrating triumphs

My parents—My solid foundation

Mum and I celebrating LIFE

Teaching mum the duckface

Me and Paul being squashed by our girls—
Aaliyah and Monique!

Cheekiness

A girls best friends

My son Jaivan . . . I owe you my life

2013

The loves of my life—my family. I couldn't have done it without you. I love you.

RESOURCES

For more information about Karina, visit her website:
http://liberation-free.com

Email: karina@liberation-free.com

Today Tonight interview:
http://www.youtube.com/watch?v=nBV3Dk9AywU

http://www.facebook.com/LiberationKarinaCarrel

http://www.twitter.com/KarinaCarrel

Dr Cali
Holistic Health of Berwick
Suite1, 16 Blackburn Square
Berwick, Victoria
03 97962100

Email: info@louiscali.com
Website: http://www.louiscali.com

Maria Kafaltis
By appointment only:

Contact: 0429 169 459
Email: souljourney@mail.com
Website: www.souljourney-visionquest.com

Dr Raj
Contact: 8802 7663 Email:
dhushyanthakumar@yahoo.com.au

For more information about blood cancers and services
The Leukaemia Foundation provide, please visit website:
http://www.leukaemia.org.au/web/index.php

★There are many centres available offering holistic
counselling services throughout Australia.

★★Facebook has a great community of groups and pages
for cancer patients and survivors.